Every school district should have copies of *Teaching School is a Scream* readily available for teachers and subs. This gave me a "shot in the arm" of enthusiasm and empowerment. It also brought back a lot of wonderful memories. Full of ideas, I can hardly wait to implement them.

~ Estela Ohashi, Substitute Teacher since 1996

Judy and I met as members of the National League of American Pen Women, Tacoma Branch. Since the aim of the NLAPW is to support fellow artists and writers, I was pleased to be a resource for Judy's book full of good advice, humor and actual classroom experiences. As an active sub my advice to teachers is this: Be friendly, firm and fair.

~ Denna J. Asbjornsen

This engaging book is filled with Judy Woods-Knight's wisdom born of experience and practical ideas coupled with emphases on the importance of humor and above all, a genuine desire to serve young minds in need of the best any teacher can deliver."

~ Gail C. Ferguson, Psychologist,
Author of *Cracking the Intuition Code*

Teaching School is a Scream!

Confessions of a Career Substitute

Judy Woods-Knight

Robert D. Reed Publishers • Bandon, Oregon

Robert D. Reed Publishers
P.O. Box 1992
Bandon, OR 97411
Phone: 541-347-9882; Fax: -9883
E-mail: 4bobreed@msn.com
Website: www.rdrpublishers.com

Cover Designer: Cleone Reed
Book Designer: Susan Leonard
Photographers: Rich Thomas for Artwork
                   Photos of Author by Yuen Lui Studio

Soft Cover ISBN: 978-1-944297-07-7
eBook ISBN: 978-1-944297-08-4

Library of Congress Control Number: 2016955987

Designed and Formatted in the United States of America

In memory of Dr. Ruth A. Willard:

A master teacher who gave her students everything she had.

Acknowledgments

My heart felt thanks go to Goldie Ann Palmer for her initial efforts on this manuscript while she was in the middle of a move. For the "heavy lifting" my thanks go to Rich and Carol Thomas who got things into the requested format. Carol, a PhD, has a gift for relentlessly scrutinizing my writing and for drawing my illustrations with flair. Rich, an engineer, is a master at the computer and the camera. It was through their efforts that this book reached Bob and Cleone Reed who own a publishing house that in 1992 published my first book: *One Thousand and One Things We Would Have Told Our Kids if They Had Ever Listened.* I am grateful to Cleone for patiently working with us and to Estela Ohashi for her help and encouragement. And, lastly, I thank my husband for his indulgence as we struggled, together, as we always have, to accomplish what often seems impossible.

Table of Contents

Preface

Who Would Do That?

Why would anyone want to become a substitute teacher? Why wouldn't a nice, accredited teacher want their own classroom and all the benefits that go along with a full-time job? How many times would a self-respecting person, someone who had worked hard for their degree allow themselves to be served "Alfredo" on a platter before a group of jeering adolescents? Or deal with little ones who are still offside with potty training? Why would anyone in their right mind allow themselves to be on several lists that could mean a call as early as 4:30 in the morning or midnight and beyond?

How about the inconvenience of being called mid-morning at the dentist's to take over for a Home Economics teacher who came down with her first, but probably not her last, migraine headache? And, the lowest call of all, how would you like to be asked at 6:00 a.m. to sub for "Field Day," i.e. the last day of school spent outdoors all day, playing games, doing relays, and eating a sack lunch in the pouring (the reason for the call) rain?

I have to admit that the reason I began subbing was that I spent our sons' college fund on a house with a swimming pool. While that is the truth, each of those sons had received an appointment to West Point and seemed to be doing well. Yet, as anyone who is even nominally acquainted with the academies knows, a student can get behind in a heart beat or be "sent home to his/her friends" for any number of reasons unrecognizable to the naked eye. Soon it became clear to me that I needed to hedge oncoming disaster and find the teacher's certificate I had recently earned and buried deep in a trunk.

The reason that I didn't want to teach school was that I didn't want to work at all. I loved the military life and was deeply dedicated to being the best military wife and the best at-home mother I could be as well. I loved moving twenty-eight times in twenty-eight years. I enjoyed decorating each of the homes in which we lived: the many mobile homes, apartments, duplexes, and army quarters we occupied. I loved cooking, cheaply and wisely for our family, and throwing dinner parties on a shoe-string. (My enthusiasm for being an at-home person was a big part of this shoe-string syndrome.) Now I look back at those early years with sadness. Our money problems and my occasional home-sickness and restlessness could have been cured by embracing what I was forced to embrace when I engineered the buying of that "dream home" in Petersburg, Virginia.

It was there that I began my fifteen years as a "career sub." In hindsight I see that subbing allowed me to have my cake and eat it too. I wish, though, that I had nibbled on it sooner. Yet now I can tell others who have a vague sense of dissatisfaction with being a "stay at homer," and a vivid dissatisfaction with never having enough money a viable way to fix their dilemmas.

My beginning salary each day was $18.75, before taxes. That amount sounds paltry but two facts surface: One, I barely deserved even that amount and two, it helped.

Today you can earn so much more than that amount that I cannot set a number. Let's just say that a friend of mine (aged 78) armed with a four-year degree recently (2016) earned $300.00 a day during a nine-week assignment for a high-school art teacher. Incidentally, I spoke with her yesterday. She's taking her husband on a cruise to Mexico.

I took my husband to Mexico on my earnings too, yet there are more compelling reasons to become a career substitute than seeing Cancun. The details follow in my story.

1. **You can own your life.** I mentioned that as a military family we moved a lot. This meant that I had to be ready to relocate at the drop of a hat. (Some school districts don't hire military spouses as full-time teachers for that reason.) But it's not just military spouses who see the benefit of owning their lives and really being there for their families.

2. **You can choose or decline a job you feel uncomfortable about taking.** (Why did I accept subbing Band? Or, why did I accept a job teaching Small Engines when I didn't know what that meant? Or Chemistry, the day we were packed for Korea?)

3. **Substitute teaching is exciting!** On a Monday I subbed a nearby kindergarten class singing little songs and reading about green eggs and ham. The very next morning at 4:30 am I was on a ferry full of grizzly looking prisoners, shackled together. Their guards were smoking and playing cards as we sailed to the infamous prison on McNeil Island. There I taught the children of the staff in a two room school house (K–2 and 3–5): a cozy little school with a potbellied stove and a picnic table outside as our lunchroom.

4. **Substitute teaching is often a humanitarian gesture.** It does your heart good to be fresh and available when a fellow teacher is ill, has a sick child or an important doctor's appointment. Sometimes the reason for their absence breaks your heart: a death, an operation, a divorce court appearance. Sometimes the teacher is just burnt out. With your enthusiasm and skill you can keep the classroom afloat until their teacher returns.

   Usually, even the sickest sounding teacher miraculously returns the next day, but not always. I innocently accepted a job in October and taught for the rest of the year.

But, I didn't have to; I was given a choice. That's the point. During that year I became more convinced than before that *I did not want a full-time teaching job, ever.*

5. **Conversely, substitute teaching gives you a chance to find a full-time job.** Doing a good job at the drop of a hat and leaving concise notes and happy students makes an impression. Not only will you have the opportunity to earn money but you will also get a chance to familiarize yourself with the various school districts; and on the basis of your stellar performance, you can choose the job you want when and if you want one.

I can tell you how. In this book I will encourage you to prepare to be a sought-after career substitute by becoming an accredited teacher first, or by augmenting any degree or part of a degree you already have earned to comply with local requirements. I will tell you how to stay fresh and enthused about your career choice and how to handle a classroom and yourself, professionally.

But there's more to the thrust of this book. Because there's a crisis for good teachers and qualified substitutes, subs are often drawn from a pool of people who have little or no college and are not prepared to return to school. Para-eds (formerly referred to as Teacher's Aides) fall into this group who, on a case-by-case basis, are hired to substitute. But others, especially in poor districts, hire those who have no college but can prove expertise in handling children. These people will be my target group in this work. I feel that if you appeal to the neediest in any group, you often offer information that will appeal to the most experienced as well. We love to see things simplified.

Enjoy my experiences: some funny, some tragic, some full of insight and skill. Others demonstrate perfect examples of bad judgment and ineptitude I worked hard to overcome. Gradually, I gained a feel for my class, any class and its mood. I also developed a stellar memory for names, a teacher's best defense. As time went on I got excited over the challenge of daring children to cooperate and have real fun learning.

PLEASE NOTE: Throughout this book, I often refer to bringing a Boom Box to school in my Toolkit. I recognize that this was the norm in my teaching days, but now a substitute teacher is more likely to bring music on a phone, an MP3 player, an iPod, or other such modern device, many of which can be hooked up to little speakers that are remarkably powerful. This way you don't have to carry several CDs with you as I did but can have a vast library of music on a very small device.

What's in Your Toolkit?

What was it about Mary Poppins that was special? Was she kind? Not overtly. Was she affectionate? Not really. Was she motherly? No. Was she professional? Yes.

That was the key to understanding what drove Mary Poppins. She had a plan. She was in control. She was one or two steps ahead of anything her little charges could throw her way. She not only had a flight plan she had options A, B, and C. Best of all, she was interesting and fun, but always on her terms. She was in charge; you can be too.

Of course Mary had magic going for her but you don't have to be magical to interject magic into a day. You can pack magic into your bag and have it at the ready.

What kind of magic do kids like? What kind of fun can a substitute teacher who isn't familiar with the schedule or the supplies at hand provide?

Remember the bag that Mary Poppins carried? It was big but not big enough to stuff in a coat rack, yet she did. Okay, you can't stuff a coat rack into your bag, but you can include a Boom Box, interesting art ideas, masters for seat games, mazes, and hand puppets. You can also pack your favorite books to read aloud or magazines or comic books to dazzle the student most bent on destroying you, and/or any classroom harmony.

You can come up with difficult "Hangman" words or "off-the-wall" guessing games to corral the most restless group. You can use inviting story-starters, exercises, songs, art projects and contests to get things going.

You can devise your own plan with options A, B, C, and D. You can pack your own Mary Poppins' bag/TOOLKIT (TK) to equip yourself for the most trying day imaginable. You can unite the group as a team to be attentive, answer questions, complete and hand in their work promptly. You've set a time on the clock or used a timer to let them know the "deadline." Then, if they have handed in their work, you will let them know what you have "up your sleeve." It might be a "cool" art project, handouts, or a seat-game. It might just be "free time:" time to talk quietly with a friend or to finish other assignments; read a magazine or carefully chosen comic books you have purchased for pennies from your favorite library; or they may just rest, as long as they stay in their seats and don't disturb other students who have not finished their work. NOTE: If they abuse this privilege, hand out seatwork as an assignment. Always be prepared with a back-up plan.

Good teachers don't just have eyes in the back of their heads; they have solutions, ways to reward or correct behavior and ways of defusing tense situations in their heads: Good teachers play chess with their students, striving to stay at least one move ahead.

Toolkit (TK) Suggestions

💼 Before you ever begin subbing, practice finding the schools in the district (s) you will be teaching. Use a GPS or a simple map to find the school, but note how long it takes to arrive at the school factoring in the weather and early morning traffic conditions.

💼 Hang season-appropriate outfits in your closet where you can grab them in a hurry. As cold as it might be at 5:30 a.m. the black turtleneck sweater you put on could be miserable at 10:00 a.m. Layer or put options in your TK.

💼 Wear a comfortable pair of shoes but pack some extra comfy shoes and dry socks.

💼 Have a lunch pail or some plastic containers ready for salad mixings and package dressings or pack lunchmeat and bread, separately, with packages of condiments. (I learned the hard way that salads wilt and sandwiches get soggy. Make your lunch fresh.)

💼 Take a beverage or two: NOT BEER as an infamous sub had done in one of my many schools. Buy a thermal container for your drinks for convenience as you might want a sip or two during the day. It's up to you whether to eat your lunch in the teachers' lounge or at your desk. I enjoyed my lunch in the classroom, alone, listening to my "Boom Box" while correcting papers, counting them against the roster for "no shows" and planning more strategy, more magic, or on bad days, dreaming of a grateful quick escape.

💼 Pack lunch money if you don't want to pack yours, and five dollars in change in case the school has a cash-lunch purchase that you handle. (We will talk about that later.)

💼 Miscellaneous but important items for your TK:

a) Cell phone and numbers of schools in which you have offered to teach as well as any other numbers important to you: hard copy or loaded on your Smart Phone.

b) A thermos you fill before you leave home and extra tea bags, if you drink tea

c) Aspirin, toothbrush, paste, gargle, floss, nail file, mirror, comb, brush, tweezers

d) Kleenex, wet-wipes, timer, airline "Sick Sacks," band aids, antiseptic, lip gloss

e) Bottled water labeled "Chill," for prizes, stickers and erasers

f) Music CDs *(Boom Box)*, appropriate DVDs

g) Hand puppets for you to use with the younger students

h) Paper plates for art projects

📋 Have masters of interesting seatwork: games, puzzles, riddles and mazes, to work; plus logos of regional teams such as the Seahawks on sheets to color. *NOTE: Jehovah Witness reject any kind of calendar celebration and their children should not be handed any seat work that reflects these holidays. Have options for them, and/or ask them what kinds of seatwork they can do, not what kind of seatwork they* **like** *to do.*

(Note) I buy packets of markers at dollar stores in case I need them (to be collected after class). In fact, for very little money I buy a lot of "treasures" there as I believe in rewards to move the day along smoothly and productively. I consider the few dollars I spend to be a small price to pay for a positive motivator; a reward for doing something award-worthy. Kids love surprises and rewards no matter how silly or small.

📋 Take something to divert yourself during your free time. **ON GOOD DAYS** I used my free time to correct papers or to dream up something to add more sparkle to our day or tally our checkbook, which often more than inspired me to do the best job I could.

📋 Be prepared **FOR NOT SO GOOD DAYS**. I suggest taking something from home that gives you joy: Load your phone with your favorite pictures, a book, a video, some music. There'll be days when a little positive reinforcement can get you ready to get things "turned around" with new confidence or remind you that there is life outside this trying classroom.

- For older kids, take a few of your old *Time* or *National Geographic* magazines; or, as I did, subscribe to a teen magazine or collect appropriate comic books. Use reading these periodicals as a reward; only if the students see this as such. As stated before, contact libraries. Some libraries sell outdated magazines inexpensively.

- The simplest and often most satisfying reward/activity is for you to read to your students from a book you think might capture their interest. Suggest they put their heads on their desk, color, or quietly do any work they feel inclined to finish. Often, you will see the students, one by one, putting aside what they were doing to listen to you. Reading in this way is calming to teacher and students and works to unify the class. If some of the class is not settling down to listen, then walk as you read until they do. Then, return to the comfort of your desk. In some of the lower grades you might encourage the students to make drawings to illustrate what the story inspires in them. Offer a prize, a sticker, or a "medal."

- Weather gear: Be prepared for rain, hail, sleet and snow, just like the mail carrier.

- Always carry sugar-free breath mints, antacids or any OTC medicine you need.

- While loading up the TK, throw in some story-starters to lighten a day or defuse tension and lighten the mood. Be inventive but expect a few groans 'til they catch on.

  a) *I won $5,000 each week for as long as I live and I can pass it on when I die:*

  b) *I won a date with Justin Bieber or Selma Gomez. What now? (G-rated answer)*

c) *It's Halloween and I wanted to do the scariest thing I could do. What was that?*

d) *Make a list of the most boring things there are to do; the most interesting?*

- Ask the class to come up with their own "story starters." Write these starters on the board. Promise a prize for the best three compositions: cursive or printed, drawings and spelling count. Set a timer for twenty minutes or more. Announce when five are left. (More story starter ideas in Appendix 2.)

- Probably the easiest and the most valuable reward you can give a student is "free-time." Use the paper cutter at school to cut bookmark sized strips of red colored paper and with a black marker write "FREE TIME." What they can do with their free time is yours to decide in each classroom you visit. You may wish to lay out the magazines and seat work that you have found appealing to their age group. (These go home with you.)

- One of the choices for grades 3–12 is "your choice as long as you aren't disturbing anyone." This gives responsible students the chance to catch up on their homework or read. Be sure to nullify the privilege if any student oversteps their bounds. You owe it to the students who do not abuse this privilege and you encourage the erring student to do better next time. Give the offender some seatwork: It's your call as to whether the seatwork will be geared towards fun or not. A quick and useful "correction" in the lower grades would be to write their next week's spelling words ten times each.

  If their offence warrants, have them use the words in a sentence. Make it clear that you mean for them to turn this assignment in to you or to their regular teacher tomorrow.

No Place to Hide

The first step is a big one. In order to begin your fascinating, challenging career as a substitute teacher, you need to contact the human resource offices of each school district in which you wish to teach. Find out if reaching their schools is feasible for you.

But first find out what their educational requirements are and any other requirements they might have. There is an enormous range of requirements from district to district so don't get discouraged if your degree is incomplete or is not in education. Work with the offices you contact as currently qualified subs are in short supply. In some cases you can work as a sub while you work on-line or on-campus to satisfy requirements you need in the long-run. You are valuable commodity!

If you are a student in pursuit of a five-year teacher's degree, you can work as a substitute in some districts. This is an invaluable experience for you and for the school as you "road test" new theories and get a "hands on feel" for the classroom as a teacher. Not only are you adding a huge dimension to your dossier you are earning substantial money to help pay for your expensive education and serving as a resource for the existing staff who might be eager to "pick your brains" as you return the favor.

Leave no stone unturned to familiarize yourself with the requirements of the job you are seeking and the pay and other benefits, if any. Be informed but get in the game.

So! You've satisfied the requirements in the schools you wish to serve. And, you've kept yourself available to field phone calls and assignments. Long ago, you had to be at home to receive a call. Now THEY CAN AND WILL FIND YOU ANYWHERE!

So, you've got a job! You're packed, clothes selected; you've loaded your lunch making ingredients and have some money; your car is gassed; you know where you're going.

You've taken care of correspondence, bills and laundry. Arrangements have been made for your kids, your spouse, your pet(s). Beds have been made. Someone has dinner figured out, (Pizza, anyone?), and you've found a safe parking space.

After a good night's sleep, a luxury you need to afford yourself: Here we go!

Before we enter the classroom, I need to bring up a controversial opinion: mine.

It is my opinion that a substitute teacher is a private entity. He or she should not attempt to get "palsy" with the full time teachers and certainly not with the principal. A good sub will go under the radar, do a good job, leave happy kids, a tidy classroom, corrected papers, a brief, comprehensive report of the day and a completed lesson plan.

Attempts to "schmooze" with the other teachers often breeds contempt. If you want their attention, do a good job: a great job. To impress a principal: never need them.

Why is this so? Because they are all busy, often overburdened.

Could it be that these people are jealous of your freedom as a career substitute?

When I taught a month shy of a full school year, I was jealous of my substitute's freedom. Maybe that's why I did what I did.

Why I Fired My Husband

The lunch count was Colonel Jim Knight's first problem: Apparently, he found it hard to handle the lunch buyers and still keep the rest of the class under control. (We are talking about fifteen students, people.)

While the sack lunch students held an informal orgy, the lunch and beverage customers stood in line, jostling one another. For reasons as yet undetermined, no one appeared with anything less than a ten or a twenty-dollar bill. Over the din created by the party going full swing in the room, Jim, slightly deaf, had trouble hearing the orders.

"Okay, you just want a beverage. Do you want 'white' milk? Chocolate? Low fat? Or skim?" Usually the student wanted orange juice or apple juice, which Jim always forgot to offer as a choice. Fortunately, the price for all the beverages was the same so he wrote down "beverage" and how much change he owed each student. (His plan was to call me during first recess to go to the bank and "get lots of change.")

Then, there was lunch. The prices for lunch varied: There was "regular lunch," "reduced lunch," and "free lunch." These students also came with large bills so the list of change I would have to get at the bank just grew and grew.

I lay in our comfortable bed, recovering from eye surgery, imagining Jim, hunched over "my" desk with a stubby pencil trying to take the count. I could hear the frantic voice I had heard so often coming over the intercom demanding the lunch count.

He didn't call me during first recess because he had duty. By lunchtime he was pretty steamed. "They kept calling over the intercom demanding my lunch count: 'MR. KNIGHT, MR. KNIGHT WE NEED YOUR LUNCH COUNT: MR. KNIGHT, MR. KNIGHT…' You'd think that the school would fall apart if my lunch count was AWOL."

I giggled slightly, before he told me I had to go to the bank.

"I forgot to tell you that 'regular lunch' and 'reduced lunch' both start with "r" so you have to write it out on the lunch tally," I reminded him, sweetly.

"What tally?" my harried husband hissed.

"The lunch tally in my top drawer. The lunch count pad I told you about right after I told you about needing tons of change."

"Oh."

"Have you handed something in yet?"

"Not exactly. After they paged me the third time I just yelled some numbers at them. I don't know if they were right. I got so hassled what with all the noise and the kid who went outside…"

"Tell Shawn 'hi' for me," I said meanly and snuggled back into my bed erroneously thinking that MR. KNIGHT would eventually get the hang of it.

He didn't. By Wednesday it was clear that I had to return, eye patch and all, or hire another sub. I couldn't do that.

We needed the money.

In his defense, I know that anytime Jim turns in a report, his taxes or any other document, it will be meticulously done, accurate and presented in a timely manner.

But not this time. No amount of coaching enabled him to do lunch count. And, truth be known, lunch count was the highlight of his day. It went downhill from there.

The tall, handsome, stern-looking full colonel, a guy who survived two tours in Viet Nam, packed parachutes, jumped out of airplanes, the guy who briefed generals and senators, earned all "A's" through graduate school, a straight arrow soldier who trained thousands of soldiers, commanded flawless parades in front of his devoted troops, all seven-thousand men and women, half of who would faint if he called them into his office, couldn't handle Ms. Knight's fifteen third graders.

But you can; you can handle anything because, unlike Jim, you have this book!

Your First Day as
a Substitute

Please forgive the seeming diversion in the last chapter. In case you missed it, I am making the point that "lunch count" is important, no matter how it is designed today.

You will see, as we go along that I will often refer to my year teaching third grade. It serves as a platform to display why full-time teaching wasn't my bag and it features valuable examples of "teaching at its best and worst and how to fix things."

Without further adieu we continue with your first day as a substitute.

You enter the school, thanking God that you found it and a good parking space and that you arrived on time. There is a certain smell to elementary and middle schools: One of sweat, spit, urine, dirt and crayons. To most dedicated teachers this smell is strangely comforting and a little exciting, in a weird way: home turf, I guess.

You give a friendly nod to the secretary/receptionist, introducing yourself, asking directions to your classroom. Then you might ask if and how you might run off some seatwork appropriate for your age group; not a lot, just thirty copies of this and that.

You enter the school office, thanking God you are on time. You sign in with the receptionist/secretary, introducing yourself and receiving the classroom key and any instructions or materials you may need to have. Sadly, this is important. If you are female you put your wallet in a desk drawer and place your purse and your TK under the desk in front of your feet. You pull out your thermos and your cup from home, oddly comforting too.

After you have written your name and the date on the board you make a quick jaunt to the teacher's lounge to store your lunch and cold beverage, nodding to the other teachers, because you are in a hurry to plan your day. NOTE: Sometimes, someone will ask whom you are replacing out of concern for one of their colleagues. If you don't remember the name of the teacher just tell them the grade you are handling.

If you did not receive a lesson plan from the office, look around the teacher's desk for one likely written under duress.

If there is no lesson plan or any other helpful material don't panic.

- **Step number one:** Place a sample of two of your seatwork on each student's desk.

- **Step number two:** Ask a reliable looking, early arriving student to assist you.

- **Step number three:** Ask for help with lunch count. (If lunch count is not a problem but you don't have a lesson plan, keep them at your desk until you schedule your day.) Keep feeding the waiting students amusing seatwork to keep order as you prepare.

1. **Do the students have their name on their desks?** (Grades 1–5) If not, after the flag salute, roll taking and announcements, hand out index cards or sticky name tags from your TK. Ask the students to write their names, then ask two students to quietly tape the cards to the desks so you can see them. Don't be tricked; check the names against the roster or seating chart.

2. **What time is recess, lunch and dismissal?**

3. **Is today a special day? Library, PE, Music, Assembly?**

4. **Do any students go to special classes?** At what time? (Ask for a raise of hands.)

5. **What is the course schedule?** Math, Reading, Spelling and so on?

6. **What page are we on in each of the text books?**

Don't Smile Until Christmas

The bell has rung. You wait for silence. This could take a century. But you wait, unsmiling. *NOTE: One teacher told me that she never smiled "until Christmas." How much did Mary Poppins or Nanny MacPhee smile? Think about it. It's easier to loosen your grip, little by little than to gain it once it's lost.*

The first day I subbed, my goal was to survive the day. Each time I subbed I would add something I had learned to my personal expectations. After a while, not only did I want to survive I wanted to keep control of myself and the class. Later I would add something that should have probably been my first goal: To accomplish what the teacher asked, or whatever I could see constituted the normal classroom day.

Over the years my objectives as a substitute formed a design familiar to everyone:

Credo:
Survive
Control
Accomplish
Unite the class
Redirect poor behavior
Reward good behavior with fun
Defuse
Defuse

What time is it now? You look at the clock as your third-grade class opens their spelling book to the appropriate page. There's a spelling test today so you allow them five minutes to take a last look at the words; suspend the study time if they are not using it well. At the end of the time you allotted, ask the class to close their books and put them in their desks.

"Does everyone have a clean sheet of paper and a pencil with an eraser? Good. I'm setting the timer for twenty minutes but if you look at the clock, the spelling test will be over at twenty minutes after nine. (This is necessary to keep things moving.)

Ask them as a group, what time is the spelling test over?"

When you clearly read the words, you have a chance to make a sentence out of each word they are to spell. I enjoy making little joke sentences... my first attempt at uniting the class. If it isn't amusing them, discontinue your efforts at levity. (Seriously.)

Once the time is up, you ask the students to exchange papers. "Make sure that your name is on your test before you exchange. Okay? Now, as a group let's spell the words correctly. Make a *small* "C" for correct by each word spelled correctly and a small check by each word improperly spelled." *NOTE: It's important to stress using discreet corrections as some students can get carried away by even this limited power.*

"Next, at the top of the paper you just corrected, *not your own paper*, in small letters write 'corrected by'* and add *your name* and the number of words they missed."

Go to the board and demonstrate what you want. Draw a page and write your name where you want them to write theirs. Show them how to discretely write numbers missed. "Is that clear?" you ask, turning around. Stay at the board and wait until the papers are passed back to their owners. (*You may use "CB" instead of "corrected by.")

"How many spelled every word correctly?" Write their names on the board. "How many only missed one word? Two words? Three words?" Reward them from your dollar store stash. *If you*

16

don't have recess duty put stickers on the papers you feel deserve recognition but only write the names of those who got everything correct on the board and hang only their papers up for display.

"Please pass your papers from the back seat to the front seat. I'm going to ask Ty to collect the papers from all five front seats and put them on my desk. Now, heads down and chill out. Until the recess bell I'm going to read Doctor Seuss's recently discovered book titled, 'What Pet Should I Get?' I think you'll like it."

If there is something else scheduled, such as reading from the *Weekly Reader*, dispense with Doctor Seuss until another time. *Always follow the lesson plan or what you have determined is the order of the day. Kids notice if you deviate and often feel uncomfortable with a change in schedule.*

You can and should use reading to settle an unruly class down. Reading is a balm to you and to your students, most of them, at any rate.

If you sense that the class is overwrought, ask them all to stand. Pull out your *Boom Box*, stick in your favorite exercise cassette and lead them in exercises. One of my favorite mentors built in seat exercises every hour of the day. It's hard to estimate the benefits of releasing some of their youthful, pent-up energy… and yours in this way.

Notice the smiles as they reach for the skies? After these exercises or in lieu of them due to time constraints, practice deep-breathing from their seats. Play something exotic on your *Boom Box*. The value of deep-breathing might be the most important lesson you teach your students all day, any day.

A Sure-Fire Art Project
(Grades 3–8)

What kid wouldn't take notice if the sub has written on the board, "'Surprise activities today!" You'll find out how your kids will feel about that if they have quietly entered the classroom after recess. (Before you dismiss them for recess, make this clear.)

If they haven't entered the classroom quietly, but have jostled and pushed one another, made a lot of noise, or knocked a desk over, wait until they are in their seats.

Quietly ask, "How many of you would like to do a special activity today?" Usually there is a lot of loud approval.

"That's good," you'll say. "But before I show you some choices I want us to practice coming in the classroom more quietly. I will dismiss you by row and you are to stand by the wall in the hall. When I come out we will walk in quietly, take our seats without jostling or punching one another or upsetting any desks. Then I will show you a special art project we can do later today."

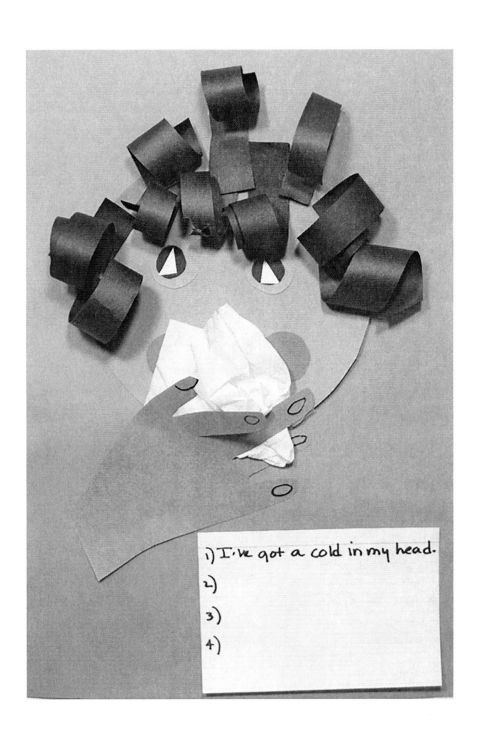

1) I've got a cold in my head.
2)
3)
4)

At this point I would show the finished product from my TK. Appendix 1 will further describe this and other worthy projects but this one deserves special mention. I like it because it involves a self portrait, "hair" made from rolling strips of colored paper around a pencil, and various other features. It will include a poem with the opening line: "I've got a cold in my head," which they are to finish.

After selecting a large sheet of paper for a background and cutting out their "face" using a small paper plate as a pattern, they will fashion eyes* from tracing around a spool of thread, and draw-on eyebrows. When this is all glued in place, they will fashion their hair using the strips of paper you have pre-cut. Show them how to roll the strips around a fat pencil, hold it until it curls. (You may dampen these strips and roll them to a pencil to facilitate the curl if you have time.) Then, when curls are dry glue one end to their "head" to create a head of hair.

Next, they are to write three more lines to rhyme with the line: "I've got a cold in my head." Use a square of white paper you have cut or index cards you have provided. Glue in place.

Then, they are to trace around their own hand, right or left, draw "U" shaped nails, (girls may want to color theirs). Glue the wrist at the bottom of the page, lightly place a tissue inside and glue a couple of fingers over the face to secure it.

The plan behind this amusing project, on a lofty level, is "self awareness." That aside, this project is fun and when completed and hung around the classroom, these happy, diverse faces and funny poems make a nice welcome back for their teacher.

This is a project best done after lunch, giving you the chance to gather the colored paper, cut the strips of paper for the "hair," blue, brown, white and black squares for the eyes that they will fashion. Set up the glue, tissue and scissors.

Because you are going to hang these pictures up, a pleasing reward is to make "ribbons" out of colored paper or ribbon with gold seals cut from paper. NOTE: I often made these at home using red and blue and green ribbon, circles of yellow colored paper with a notary seal on top. The result is worth the effort.

Relax and try to enjoy your lunch; it's going to be a busy afternoon.

Make sure you do everything the teacher expected you to accomplish. You can move the day along with the reminder, "Whether or not we get to do the art project depends on doing a good job with our morning work." (These reminders should be done cheerfully, nobody likes to be nagged.)

In Appendix 2 I will list a number of other interesting art projects suited to a one day or two day teaching assignment.

It is my experience that art projects are worth the effort because:

1. They don't happen unless the class has been productive.

2. They unify the class to a common goal.

3. They give a student a chance to "shine" who might not, otherwise.

4. They serve as tension relievers (for the students, at least).

5. The end result can brighten even the dreariest classroom.

6. A successful art project makes you feel good, especially this one.

It works best to have a sample of any art project you are introducing. Not only does it save time, it inspires your students to be creative, often coming up with a better finished product than the one you presented.

To facilitate any art project be sure that you have plenty of 7" paper plates, spools, of thread and Mason jar lids in your TK. Cutting circles is difficult and time-consuming.

Usually there is a box of tissue in the classroom but bring your own just in case.

*A special note reference the eyes: To make them stand out and sparkle, trace around a penny or a dime on black paper. Glue it to the eye. Then cut out a small triangle from a scrap of white paper, or a circle from a paper punch and position it in the same angle on each eye. Students can look at the sample you provided for guidance.

What to Do When You Don't Know What to Do
(Part 1)

(Grades 7–12)

It's pretty obvious that there is a big difference between teaching grades 1–5, 6–9 and 10–12. And, it's assumable that most teachers have a preference or at least a "comfort zone." But, as a substitute, you might often be called upon to manage a class outside your comfort zone. Let's tackle such a day together.

Let's accept a tenth-grade math class. (I know.)

Jerome bursts through the door and slings his books on his front row desk, knocking over his chair. Without picking it up he asks, "Who are you?"

Calmly, you grab one of the "free time" red tabs you pulled from your TK before you stowed it expecting a need.

"Pardon me?" you ask, nicely giving Jerome a chance to politely ask your name.

He doesn't. In fact he is more insolent than before, repeating the question.

"My name is on the board," you say calmly. "Please come to the desk." (I avoided saying "my desk" because I am a visitor.)

"Do you see this red tab?"

"Yes."

"What does it say?"

"It says 'free time.'"

"That's right. Would you like to have some free time to do what you want if you finish your work? I've got some comic books and some cool puzzles and games…"

"Sure."

"Good. I want you to straighten the desk, pick up the chair that fell over, gather up your books and go into the hall and come back in like the gentleman I know you can be. And, I'd like it if you would greet me politely. Do you think you can do all that?"

"I dunno."

Begin to put the red strips away.

"Yeah, I guess I could do that."

"Good, I hoped you would."

At no time did you raise your voice or scold him. You simply offered him a few options that you felt would be tempting. You also complimented him by suggesting that you knew *that he could be a gentleman and by suggesting that the chair simply fell over.*

The next hour, Nordonne comes in and slings his books around and knocks his chair over. You notice that Nordonne is as big as a bear as he growls "Who are you?"

You bring him to the desk and offer him the same deal that you had offered Jerome. His answer is different:

"I don't plan to hand in my work so I don't need no 'free pass.'"

"That's your choice. I will have another option for you so please pick up your chair and take your seat. You and I will talk after I get the rest of the class settled in."

Again, you have controlled your voice. You have not quarreled with him or even confronted him, and you have offered him other options while treating him with respect.

After you have presented the lesson you hand any paperwork assignment to the first seats to pass back. Nordonne throws his on the floor.

"I don't have to do this crap," he says.

You say nothing. You don't even ask him to pick up the paper he discarded. You go into your TK and pull out a questionnaire that you have at the ready for the Nordonnes you might encounter. (A copy of such a document will be in Appendix 1.) The idea is to defuse his anger by finding out what's bothering him, not that his behavior is bothering you. Through your questionnaire you will keep him busy defusing the situation.

If Sophia says, "Why doesn't Nordonne have to do his math like we do?"

"That's a really fair question but this is between Nordonne and me. If you feel you need to know more about it, you can see me after class."

"Can I do the same paper as he?"

"Yes, but you have to do your assignment first."

"He doesn't."

"Oh yes. Nordonne will be responsible for handing in this assignment tomorrow."

Usually that approach satisfies the "Sophia's" and usually they do not follow up on wishing to have the same assignment as you have given Nordonne. If she turns up with her assignment finished, glance at it to see if she has done a good job. If she has, give her or anyone else who presses the matter a copy of the *"I'm having a bad day document."*

The document I am presenting is anonymous, non-confrontational, sympathetic and even therapeutic for some one who's having a bad day. (Besides you.) And it works.

For the older students, interesting seatwork is an extremely valuable tool. So are magazines and carefully selected comic books. Almost every student appreciates "free-time." You can tell if free time is productive or not. If not, seat work is a good option.

With upper grades, don't try to be their buddy. Take roll, teach what is to be taught, monitor the group fairly, grade their papers and leave with your self-esteem intact.

A Labor of Love?

At first, I suffered anxious hours as I waited for the phone to ring calling me to work. Yet, I used the time to critique my efforts. Some of the time I scolded myself for not handling a situation well, other times I congratulated myself on a good job and there were also a few times that I came up with "brilliant" approaches to conflicts, solutions or something as simple and concrete as a new seat game, a puzzle or a nifty art project.

Yet, I badly needed a project to keep me busy as I waited for the phone to ring. I needed something useful to do as I wrestled with myself trying to dig deep inside me to come up with ways to best teach school and to defuse the anger I sometimes saw in my students *and* myself as we tried to achieve our goals. (People: Driving a sub crazy is often a primary goal.)

Soon after moving into our new house in Virginia I discovered a not so tiny flaw in my "dream home." I was crushed to realize that the paint on every inch of woodwork throughout the 2,700 square feet in our home was chipping way to reveal that the former owner had covered white enamel paint with jade-colored acrylic paint. (They don't bond.)

As I sanded and later painted I thought about how I could be a better teacher, how I would handle rudeness professionally, how I could smoothly defuse bad situations, how I could handle disasters large and small, and how I could quickly earn my students' respect. I admit it, looking for these answers was often frustrating but I took out that frustration on the doors, the baseboards and window sills, even the wainscoting in the dining room. Nothing escaped my aggressive sanding and painting fueled by my angst.

During this time, I accepted many calls to teach inner city kids in Petersburg, a challenge I performed with varying degrees of success.

I would learn that if you hadn't received a call by eleven o'clock, am, you still weren't "off the hook." You might receive a "half-day" assignment at noon and need to rush to conduct a class through the second half of the day. I did this frequently *because I was available and enthusiastic.*

Slowly but surely, the sanding was accomplished and so was the painting. I was proud of the hours of merciless introspection, answering every call to teach with a range of success, and the wood work with an even wider range of accomplishment.

Rightly or wrongly, I am not a *detail* person. Mine is the *broad brush approach.*

This preference would serve me well in another project that is a struggle for me even though it involves a broad brush.

Next to sanding and painting, I hate hanging wallpaper. I have a fighting chance with sanding and painting but wallpapering is beyond my scope.

So, let's do this.

Another Chance to Excel

Question: Why did I choose to wallpaper the upstairs bathroom?

Two reasons: One, I actively hated the existing wallpaper and two, the offensive area was very small.

It was spring. John was a Yearling (sophomore) and Jim a Cow (junior).

Once again we had decided to drive the nine-hour drive from Petersburg to West Point, an hour out of New York City. The boys seemed to enjoy our visits.

Usually, I was excited to make the trip, but this time I was busy hanging the wallpaper and didn't have my heart in the long drive.

The night before we left, I packed and prepared "Boodle" (snacky things). In fact, I did all of the things I did as loving mother before I became a "Wallpaper Nazi."

Then, right before bedtime I carefully hung, according to instructions, the pre-cut wallpaper: a pretty pink background with little white valentine hearts. (You'd love it.)

In the morning, to my horror, the wall paper lay crumbled in misery in the tub.

There was no time to do anything so I closed the door, hoping no one would see, and left.

We always brought our sweet dog. We had to smuggle Maggie into the cheap motel where we stayed thinking, erroneously, the manager wouldn't notice or care.

The trip was painful on so many levels: Jeff, a fourth grader, hated long car trips as much as I. Jim had tennis elbow and suffered through the eight zillion salutes a LTC has to return when in uniform. On a less lofty level, I mourned my wallpaper.

We did all the usual things and were appropriately inspired by the magnificence of just about everything. *(Except for moi.)* I even gagged as one of our boys told me an often quoted refrain: *Everyday at West Point is a new chance to excel.* (Oh, please!)

My mood went from skepticism to outright hostility, to a feeling of unworthiness, followed by a feeling of anxiousness, concluding in a full-blown, four-star-anxiety attack.

We were in the enormous dining hall where thousands are fed at one time. Birds flew overhead, pooping at will. I felt uncomfortable and ill at ease just being there.

When you are having an anxiety attack you think of things like this and remember what your sons went through during their entire Plebe years, eating "square meals." This meant they had to put food into their mouths at square angles accounting for the huge cleaning bills during that time period as well as their significant weight loss.

My mind was on fire as my eyes darted around looking for comfort. Everyone looked so intelligent, so in control, so capable of all things to include hanging wallpaper.

I sat in misery, hating myself while daring a bird to poop on my plate.

Just then a good-looking guy across from me, wearing a polo shirt introduced himself. "Hi, I'm Ted."

I returned with my introduction and, in spite of myself, I gave him a chance to divert me. After a few pleasantries I casually asked Ted what he did for a living.

"I'm a wallpaper hanger," he answered.

In a short but meaningful conversation, my new best friend told me what to do.

"Soak the paper in warm water for a few hours and re-hang it. Use a broad brush or a roller to smooth it out. It'll be fine; I promise you."

I learned something else valuable: *Everyday really can be a new chance to excel.*

The Gentleness of
a Country School

I know I need to talk about this as it has affected my life and made me who I am.

When I was sixteen years old, my mother gave birth to a daughter with Down syndrome. A lot of people will tell you how blessed you are to have such a child; but to me the event, then and now, had all the charm of unplugging life's Christmas tree.

It worried me to wonder how I would deal with a handicapped class. I had some experience dealing with Julie and the various "baby schools" she attended. but I didn't know how well I could stand up against expectations, having not solved my own grief.

"Ms. Knight? Are you free to go to Prince George County to take over a handicapped class tomorrow?" I was about to find out if I could handle the emotional turmoil.

It was a long way there, but a pretty drive. I love Virginia. We might have retired there had it not been for family on the west coast: Jim's and mine. And Julie.

I entered the classroom and was followed by the principal who looked a little like Hugh Grant. Having an escort was unusual, I thought to myself, feeling uncomfortable.

Mr. Pace opened the door for me—even more than unusual. I was soon to see that he had the kind of hesitant charm that had made Hugh Grant famous and hugely rich.

"Um," he said, hedging a bit trying to tell me in his *hugh-grantianway* that one of my students was really special.

31

"Brandon is a singular child," he began. (Oops, teacher-talk.)

"Okay?" I said, exhibiting no special reactions.

"He is blind, deaf, and incontinent, at least most of the time."

"I can deal with that," I answered, ever the good Campfire girl.

"But there's more," he said, sitting, lowering his head and looking at his hands.

"Oh?" I asked, looking at the clock dwindle down and with it my prep time.

"Brandon communicates with the world with his tongue; can you deal with that?"

Just then the bell rang, Mr. Pace jumped up, and my answer was lost in the mists.

"Hi there," the short, perky aide said as the principal left through the door of my currant classroom. Edie was a brunette, with "brunetty" natural charm.

I wanted to ask her about Brandon, but all of a sudden there was too much going on as one handicapped child after another was lead into our midst. I was struck with an overwhelming feeling of inadequacy that I had never felt before. What was I supposed to do with all of these kids?"

I looked at the lesson plan.

It was vague: heavy on "play activities," "circles," and a whole lot of "ask Edie's."

Out of nowhere, Brandon arrived looking well-cared for in his bright red Buster Brown shorts and a striped top, the set our boys used to wear. He was on the tall side for kindergarten, slim and tanned, as though he had been outside a lot. His smart crew cut displayed a handsomely shaped head and cleanliness to put most mothers to shame.

It was clear that he was blind but deafness doesn't show, not right away. Edie handled him deftly while I checked in the rest of our twelve special students.

Gathering together in the first of many circle times, I gently explained who I was. As we launched into a low-key introductory exchange, I tried to assess each student.

Out of the corner of my eye I saw Edie setting Brandon on a potty chair. She was gentle but firm with him and helped him sit down. To my knowledge he stayed there for the rest of the class with only a break at recess and lunch.

With the help of my aide, we attended to our students as best as we could, which is to say that we kept them safe and occupied. After each circle time I gave them "play time," and each child excitedly headed for familiar toys and time with their friends. I hated to interrupt their fun but needed to follow the teacher's lesson plan.

Wouldn't you know that I HAD RECESS DUTY? I was crestfallen as I really needed a cup of hot tea and a chance to collect myself. Nevertheless, I entered the play area dominated by a huge oak tree, hundreds of years old. The tree comforted me.

The air smelled of blossoms and a gentle, warm breeze gave a little lift to my anxious spirits. As I had suspected, seeing so many children who had a limited future had proven traumatic for me. Why?

Mr. Pace was outside too, something I had rarely seen: a principal involved in recess? He was talking to the children and the other teacher on duty.

And then I saw Brandon. He approached the oak tree and licked it. I was close enough to see that his tongue was not like his classmate's tongue or any other tongue that I had observed. His tongue was strong and hard, and he thrust it out again and again like a lizard. He had a firm grasp on the tree and was hard at work. It was horrifying to me.

The principal came toward me. I must have looked appalled as he soothingly explained that due to his sensory deprivations (more teacher talk) he uses his tongue to explore the world around him.

"Has he approached you?" Mr. Pace asked.

"No," I replied trying not to shudder. "As a matter of fact, Edie has had him on the potty chair all morning. I guess there's a 'major press' to get him toilet trained."

He laughed, gently. "Ah yes, potty training. A very time-consuming venture in some cases, but always a major accomplishment. Are you okay?"

"Yes," I'm okay," I lied as the bell rang to return to class. "I'm good."

During the rest of the day my aide shared more and more information with me about my students—not gossip or complaints—just things I needed to know to better reach them, deal with them. I appreciated her help. Together, we gave each student our best.

After the children were collected I sat at the desk and Edie drew up a chair, facing my desk. "I'd like to explain a little about Brandon; is that okay?"

"Sure," I said, sitting back, appreciating that aides didn't often offer information about the children in special classes, unless specifically asked by the substitute.

"His mom and dad were high school sweethearts. They got engaged and she got pregnant. She got German measles, the baby was born afflicted, and the dad bailed."

As I was pondering these sad facts and about to torture myself with pity for Brandon's mother, I remembered her as she had been when she came to pick up her son.

She was young and very pretty, but when she laid eyes on Brandon, she lit up like the Christmas tree I had unplugged for myself so long ago.

She scooped her boy into her arms, hugging him close to her, kissing his cheeks as though he were the joy of her life.

He was.

I know.

I really do.

Romancing a Stone

My time in the inner-city middle school classes in Petersburg continued to be a trial and terror experience: heavy on the trial and on the terror. It seemed as if no amount of preparation on my part improved my relationship with my students. Of course I blamed "reverse prejudice," but call it what you like, I was being paid to do a job and I wasn't succeeding.

Looking back, I see that many of the tips, insights, and suggestions that I am offering in this book were learned there, where instead of being easier to teach, as I erroneously thought they would be, the kids in that impoverished area were harder to teach, harder to reach.

Kids in impoverished areas do not always have parental support or, in some cases, even adequate supervision. And on their own, these kids do not often see education as a way out of poverty. In fact, some families think of welfare as the family business in a *get even/we deserve this* manner. My husband as a commander would see this attitude in his troops as well. Young soldiers would turn down re-enlistments or promotions to join the rest of their family on welfare. (Happily, this is not the norm.)

In exasperation, I lashed out at a classroom full of boys who were indifferent to the assignment I had handed out. No, that sounds too sterile. Let's just say that a group of belligerent boys refused to do the assignment because "they just didn't want to do it."

Let's be clear about something important: There are the students who quietly do not do their work, sliding, undetected under the radar; and then there are the in-your-face variety challenging you to get them to do anything other than disrupt the classroom and show off.

Still remembering my day at Prince George, I turned the lights off and asked everyone to sit down and listen to me. I waited a long time for silence, dealt with a couple of fist fights, suffered through insults being hurled my way, and snatched one chap who was about to stroll out the door.

Whether or not what I had to say made any impression, I do not know. But, I know that I hit home with one or two students when I told them about the students I taught who have little or no chance for a bright future because they are handicapped.

I tried to make the point that everyone in this math class is able-bodied and bright. That "nothing stands in your way to do anything you want to do." That instead of hating school and disrespecting their teachers and ignoring their assignments that they might instead look at the very schools they trash and the teachers they abuse as their way out, their way up, their ticket to a happier life.

Because I was so new and so inept, my effort could be filed under "LECTURE." Nobody likes a lecture, but mine came from the heart and was intended to help them. Perhaps that is the intention of every lecture and rarely do we succeed.

Today, I might have given out the same information but in a different form. I would have said: "I am going to tell you a story and after I have finished, I want you to write down as much as you remember about what I said and what it means to you.

"After twenty minutes, we will have a group discussion about what we wrote. If it's productive, we'll have 'Free Time' from 2:30 until dismissal."

That's how you turn things around and defuse a nasty situation.

But I did none of those things. I hadn't learned how to defuse a situation. Instead I pouted, ranted and raved, and demanded cooperation from a stone, knowing that since I had accepted a two-day assignment, tomorrow would be even worse than today.

The odd thing was this: Ms. Green, the black principal had faith in me. I felt as though I was letting her down, along with myself and my students, but I kept trying.

Sometimes the mere effort of trying is all you can do.

Monica

When I got home, I called a friend of mine who is a master teacher. Sandy listened to me and gave me advice that sounded helpful. I took it to heart.

After a restless night, I felt more unable than ever as I stood before first-period Math. The usual carnival was going on among the "Back Row Boys." The first few rows were reasonably quiet, ready to listen to what I had to say. Or, were they just apathetic?

Armed with the tips Sandy had given me, I stood, still and motionless, waiting for silence. From where I stood, I could see my car, a connection with real life where, like a soldier in combat, I didn't have to fight for every inch of ground. Looking at my dear car made my eyes sting with tears.

It took what seemed like ten-and-a half years of waiting, but it finally happened, out of curiosity, I suppose. The "Back Row Boys" sat down and actually looked at me.

Just as class seemed ready to say the flag salute, Monica, a beautiful, respectful girl with the body and grace of a ballerina, passed a note.

Because I was practicing strictness I felt that I couldn't play favorites, and that I would have to chastise Monica for passing a note *right in front of my eyes.*

What ever propelled me to try to make a joke of it? What was I thinking when I said; "Oh class, Monica has something she would like you all to know."

It worked. I had them. For the first time in forever, all eyes were on me, hanging on what I had to say. I felt victorious, one of them: *accepted*. Fortunately, for all of us, I read the note silently first. It said: "I wish Ms. Knight was my mother."

I folded the note, composed myself, and when I could speak I whispered to Monica, "I'd like that too."

Then I quietly announced that I was wrong. Monica's note had been private and that it was time to stand for the "Pledge of Allegiance."

First recess I went to my car and cried and cried. I recognized that as a teacher I was at least scoring points as a good mother.

Yet, it was about this time that I came up with an idea. I came up with a plan to help boys and girls who have for whatever reason given up: No matter how belligerent they are or how few assignments they turn in, assign them as mentors to students who are less capable than they.

Trust them to listen to these kids read or practice their math skills.

Let them see what it is to work with a student who is not working to potential. Let them feel responsible for someone else. Let them feel the frustration you and other teachers feel with a student who has "checked out" or who has never "checked in."

At first, the older student will relish the opportunity to "get out of work" to "get over" to monitor other students. But, it won't take long before they see what it is they are supposed to see.

There is monumental tragedy and waste in a fully capable yet indifferent student. It takes patience and endurance for a caring teacher to encourage them to do better.

What to Do When You Don't Know What to Do
(Part 2)

(Handicapped, Special Ed, and Gifted)

In a perfect world, we wouldn't have Handicapped or Special Needs classes; we also wouldn't have sick teachers or have to ask a substitute teacher to be prepared to teach School-Funded Day Care, Pre-Kindergarten, Kindergarten, 1–12, Gifted, Library, PE, Music, Choir, Home Economic, Small Engines, Shop, Shakespeare, Sociology, Chemistry, Math, Algebra, Geometry, Trig, or Sociology, yet those were some of my assignments.

Also, we wouldn't have burnt out teachers or teachers who have emergencies dire enough to call on a substitute. We wouldn't have teachers who had to teach even if they didn't like teaching. We wouldn't have single moms who need/want to stay home with their little ones but have no other means of support; teachers who are too old or too infirmed to teach but need to earn their retirement; teachers who are disillusioned in their work but have earned tenure though they do not deserve it.

Then we have desperate men or women who can't find a job that they are better suited for than teaching. And people who might think that teaching school is easy or, worse yet, beneath them. Then, there are people with huge mortgages, alimony bills, or illness in the family that makes the insurance side of teaching school attractive even if the job is not.

You, as a substitute have the chance to be a superhero coming in to save the day! Okay, most days you are simply holding down the fort, but bring your cape along anyway; and we'll talk about what you can do to keep an even keel even when things go sideways.

Rule # one: Follow the lesson plan. If AWOL, have the PE help you write one.

Handicapped

Normally there is a PE (Para-Ed) in your class to help you. If you are having trouble in Handicapped, you will need to rely on their help because the needs of these students can have a wide scope and a misstep could get you in huge trouble.

Many of the students under your supervision will require intense personal care, even for students in their teens. You need to put on your Superman cape and do what you have to do. It might not be the most glamorous part of teaching school, but with humility and charity, change that diaper, happy that you are able to do what the state is mandated to do: provide appropriate education for all its children.

While you are attempting to educate their children, or at least provide a safe, new experience, you are giving the parents or guardians of these children a break from the never-ending challenge of caring for them around the clock. It would be virtually impossible to measure what any of these students is gaining from their school experience. In the case of CP (cerebral palsy), you would be surprised as in so many other handicaps.

What to do when you feel "freaked" or exhausted and out of your depth handling a handicapped class?

Pull out your *Boom Box* and play something uplifting, something you think they would like (after your careful research and recording or collecting age and capability appropriate music for all the levels you might teach). I especially like "Itsy Bitsy Spider" by Carly Simon for Handicapped, Special Ed and Pre-K-3; but all groups enjoy the song.

Then, gather those who are gatherable (sometimes students are brought in on gurneys) into a circle. It there are young children, pull out a hand puppet and go person to person asking each student his or her name; ham it up, you and the puppet.

Interact with each child. Do calendar, flag, sing a song or two. Play guessing games or play "Button Button." Usually twenty minutes of teacher-led circle is enough. Dismiss them one by one to their desks or areas. Get back to the lesson plan or read to them, asking those who can, to draw a picture your story suggests to them. If you have deaf kids, get them back on track with what the teacher had planned or ask the PE to help out.

If the PE is busy or if there are no guidelines, give non-verbal instructions for them concerning a picture they might draw *as an assignment* or let them have free play time, always a safe bet in a Handicapped or Special Ed class. (You might unwittingly create resentment expecting a blind child to draw or a deaf child to listen to you read.)

While some of what I have written may sound daunting, the day can be especially rewarding for you. As mentioned, in contrast to some students in other grades who are disruptive in class and show little appreciation for your efforts or for the opportunities education affords, these handicapped kids appreciate their teachers and school. Teaching them might be a rewarding experience as these kids are often easier to please.

Or, like me, you might get fired (details in Chapter 14).

Special Ed

Okay! What do you to do when everything falls apart in Special Ed? (We are talking about kids crying, wandering around, whining, hitting one another, biting or throwing toys, talking back.) Here again you will likely have a Para-Ed trained to follow the daily routine who will assist you, when and if you request help; yet they are usually concerned with the most difficult children to smooth the way for the teacher to work with the students who would most benefit from his/her instruction.

But now you are in crisis mode. You dim the lights and raise your hands, while encouraging them to do the same as you sing a song that smacks of "clean-up time or" chill-out time." Call for circle, once more, and gather them to you. Because they have acted up, you might use your hand puppet again and talk about the rules that you saw being abused. In a friendly way you will ask the puppet if throwing things in class is okay. Hitting? Biting? (You get the picture.) Normally, this effort defuses the situation without scolding or singling the offending student(s) out, and you have made your point, smoothly.

Depending on what time it is and/or how much of the lesson plan has been accomplished, you can use this circle time to play a guessing game or *tell* a story, *locking eyes with them* to show them that you are in control of yourself *and* the situation.

Then slowly but surely, ease them, one at a time, away from circle to their desks and the work at hand or play time. Perhaps heads down and read a story or sing a song.

While walking around the class, you are zeroing in on any student who is being disruptive by standing over his/her desk as you read or sing. After you have sung enough verses of "The Wheels on the Bus Go Round and Round" or another song from Appendix 2, return to the lesson plan refreshed.

Promise another story later if there's time. (Use books already in room as some schools control what is read.)

But, if pandemonium breaks out again, go for another circle. This time try singing something that involves hand gestures such as "Itsy Bitsy Spider," which is always a feel-good song for student and teacher alike, especially if you have the music on your *Boom Box.*

Gifted

I wince even writing that word that once applied to students who seemed to have a gift for learning. I found them a very difficult group to teach because I hadn't given them enough thought. There is a challenge in this class: trying to interest them without feeling the compulsion to exhibit your own "giftedness" is tricky.

If the teacher has left a lesson plan and if the students are applying themselves, simply address the lesson plan. If they are rowdy, disrespectful, and/or bouncing off the walls, solve this dilemma by having a special set of story starters for these bright kids in your TK. *Hint: don't get lofty. Super bright students see right through any efforts towards pandering.*

Story starter ideas? See the following (200 words or more):

1. Considering world hunger: *How do you feel about the cafeteria food?*

2. What course(s) caused you to wonder *why am I taking this?*

3. Who was your favorite, least favorite teacher and why? (No names, please.)

4. Discuss and defend your favorite movie, TV program, book, play, music, sport.

5. Why should you be allowed (not allowed) to use your phones in the classroom?

6. Choose your own subject.

Impress on the students that these are neither games nor are they optional exercises. Their efforts will be handed in, graded, and "rewarded." (Even smart kids like prizes.)

Stress that these essays should contain two hundred words, that they may write on more than one subject, and but they need to write a minimum of 200 words. If you think they would appreciate your gesture (softly) play "Kodachrome" by Paul Simon as they write.

The song is usually accepted gleefully. Be specific with them; they can be super critical.

Play "Hangman" with this group, challenging each student to come to the board and monitor their specific word. You might demonstrate by starting with "Czechoslovakia."

Reward good work from your stash of magazines ("Time" is good for this group) or Sudoku puzzles geared to the Mensa Class. Surprisingly they like comic books too, carefully chosen by you or the library where you bought them second hand for cheap.

As you usually have these students for only one period, these classes can be fun.

I will return with more solutions for what to do when you don't know what to do.

In Chapter nineteen we will address survival techniques for grades Pre K–12.

But before we leave this chapter. I want to talk about an assignment that still leaves me unable to adequately describe its difficulty. I lived through it; and you will live through difficult assignments too, if you are flexible, calm, and creative, knowing that you don't have to do this tomorrow. Usually.

Before I describe this assignment, it is necessary for me to admit that I have no sense of direction. In fact, I could get lost on a bridge.

Yet, in an age, before GPS's and other devices to help the "directionally challenged," I managed to arrive at my assignments on time albeit with great difficulties.

I accepted an assignment that sounded okay: teaching music. I had no idea that this meant driving from one to four additional schools each day, nor did I understand, at least initially, that this assignment was a week long. Just finding five schools in one day would often be challenge enough for me, forget about teaching music.

Add to that, the fact that there would be no lesson plan, no piano, no song book, no tattered pages of music, not even a drum or a stick to beat the cadence of my despair.

Suffice to say that in Appendix 2 of this book you will find a plethora of songs and CDs geared to an exhausted, well-meaning music substitute teacher, sans equipment.

Did you know that with your Boom Box playing alluring Samba, Hawaiian, or Rap music, kids can beat their desks like drums with their hands? That you can create an "orchestra" in your classroom by dividing the kids into groups beating on chairs, desks and anything you can find to exclude one another. (I didn't think of it at that time, either.)

I refer to a "Boom Box" often. That was the way to bring music to the class when I was substituting. You probably have music on your phone, an iPod, an MP3 player, or other such device with small speakers that play big. The point is that having music at your fingertips at any moment that you want is crucial to your success.

As I write these pages it suddenly occurs to me why I got involved in so many classes that presented seemingly insurmountable problems. It has nothing to do with my reputation or my skill. They call you so early or so late that you can't defend yourself appropriately and often you don't ask the right questions.

"What's a small engine?" Anyone? Anyone?

A Couple of Sour Notes

During this time, our whole family was struggling to a greater or a lesser degree. My husband, Jim, was succeeding, usually, learning how to manage, encourage, and inspire the men and women in his battalion. Third grader son Jeff was struggling to learn how to adapt to the rigors of a Catholic school.

Sons Jim and John had a range of experiences at the Academy, and I never lost sight of the fact that they could fall like a house full of cards at any time.

This last thought kept me struggling to do my best as a substitute teacher.

Often I would stagger home, tired from a demanding day to take a phone call from one or the other son sounding lost, sad, worried, angry, homesick, or semi-hysterical.

I would sink into our rocking chair, the chair in which I fed all three their baby bottles. As I rocked, I listened to their problems and tried to "talk one or the other cadet out of a tree." Chemistry was often a troublesome subject as was physics, not to mention interminable hours spent marching and standing in formation eating up their study time.

At that time reverse charge, long-distance calls were expensive. And, since our conversations were often lengthy, there were more than a few occasions when our talks exceeded what I earned that day. I never regretted the chance to talk and encourage them.

Encouragement for me was of a different ilk. If the phone kept ringing for me, I felt as though I was growing a reputation. I looked at frequent calls as approval.

But then, I need to speak of *that* day when my reward was termination.

I can still see the mini-ambulance bringing one of my "students" in on a gurney. She was apparently age appropriate to my assigned class, but she looked at least twenty-five to me. Then, there were several other severely handicapped, large students for me and my PE to manage.

The day was hectic and difficult. At one point I was obliged to change a diaper on "Melissa," another full-grown female student.

The diaper was too small for her and caused me a lot of difficulty, finally solved by using masking tape to secure it. Melissa was sweet and understanding as I struggled.

Before the end of the day I wrote a short note to go home with Melissa, commenting on her sweetness and sharing the fact that I had a sister with Down syndrome so I understood the joys and sorrows families with handicapped children feel.

Then, I suggested to her parents that she needed larger-sized diapers.

Now, I realize why I got fired. (Have I stressed often enough that *substitutes need to travel under the radar?*) I wish I had this book then. I was wrong to do that. If I thought the child should have larger diapers, I should have left a note *for the teacher* to that effect. I overstepped my bounds in writing directly to the parent. Although I did apologize, the principal did not accept my apology and was adamant that *I was fired.*

I was called to teach in that school again and I went. I don't think anyone knew of my mistake or, indeed, that I was even there. (Guess I understood the radar thing.)

The following is a far different situation which I will attempt to describe fairly. Decide for yourself. Did I have reason to complain even though I might lose future assignments? Was I right to stay below the radar simmering with anger? You decide, remembering that you, as a substitute teacher have a right to fair treatment.

Dilemma

It was a pretty spring day, the kind of day that makes many students "antsy." I was called to a familiar school to sub for fifth graders. I knew the students well.

As I looked at the lesson plan and gloried in the fact that because these students were about to go to middle school, the principal from their current elementary school and the principal of their new middle school would spend forty-minutes talking about making a smooth transition. I envisioned the large block of time, sitting at my desk watching a couple of ultra-successful, dedicated male teachers in action, knocking 'em dead with caring and insight over the student's possible feelings of anxiety about this transition.

WHAT I SAW ASTONISHED ME: The students were noisy, rude, inattentive, and insolent as these two men tried to assure them that they would be welcomed into their new school in the fall. As I sat there in disbelief, I wanted to stand and announce that these students wouldn't be welcomed into a juvenile detention house acting like this. I sat simmering for the entire forty minutes as neither man called for order or chastised the group for their inattention. I couldn't wait for this atrocity to end. (Picture Tina Fey.)

When their visit finally ended and after I had graciously thanked the two men for their time, I dimmed the lights. It was recess time and the class was anxious to go: so was I because I had duty.

"What were you thinking?" I asked softly? "Why were you so rude to not one but two principals who were trying to make you feel better about going to middle school? I am ashamed of you. You don't appear ready to go to middle school to me. If I didn't have duty, you'd be denied recess since you deserve neither middle school nor recess."

Reluctantly, I excused them row by row and with a heavy heart went outside. As usual, I was surrounded by a circle of girls who want to hug the teacher, any teacher. I had/have no illusions about this. They were probably just chilly or bored. I know this because the minute we entered the classroom their attitude towards me took a nosedive.

And then, from nowhere, comes a rock. It hits my forehead. I ignore it, because, God help me, I love the touch of my little group of fans. We move en masse to another spot where I hope my attacker will not find me. He finds me, and this time I identify him as one of the agitators against the principals. This time the rock grazes my ear. My little girlfriends don't notice my distress, and we move again into the bright sun giving Jerome a perfect chance to throw a bigger rock and hit me dead between the eyes, breaking the bridge of my relatively new three hundred seventy-five dollar tri-focal sunglasses.

Recess is suddenly over! The students line up waiting for me to dismiss them. After I saw straight lines and no pushing or shoving, I called: "Ms. Stewart's class may go. Ms. Palmer's class may go. Ms. Cook's class may go. My class may go."

We get into the warmth of the classroom. I wrote an assignment on the board—a few pages of reading from their often ignored social studies text. I then assigned a "class monitor." Then, I confronted Jerome. (Since this is the first and only time I had taken a child to the principal, I wasn't sure what the procedure was.)

He resisted. I insisted, and before you know it we were standing in front of the same principal who that morning had demonstrated his classroom management style.

I stated my case, simply, and left, anxious to return to my students.

The rest of the day was sad for me. I had never had to resort to this extent to manage my teaching day. Yet, I had given this student several opportunities to stop throwing rocks at my face and head. He had rejected his opportunities. So I seized mine.

All day long I had expected some kind of restitution, if not for me, for my glasses. I felt that I was the wounded one. I felt that I had dealt with the situation professionally.

At the end of the day I wrote a note to the teacher minimizing the trauma I felt and putting the best spin on the day that I felt to be appropriate. I ached to go home.

Over the intercom came the call I had expected all day. "Ms. Knight, please come to the principal's office."

Probably for effect, I wore my sunglasses, fastened now with tape from my TK. The effort was wasted, I would soon learn.

I stood before the man who had come in second to last against a group of fifth graders. I wasn't asked to sit nor was I greeted in a friendly way.

"I didn't like the way you handled today's *little incident*," he said.

My eyes stung behind my taped sunglasses. "Why?" I asked.

Shifting in his chair, he replied, "I heard from some of Jerome's classmates that you boasted the rest of the day that you got him expelled."

"Well, first of all, I did not know that Jerome was expelled. I only knew that he was no longer in my classroom. I was heart-broken over this ugly incident and never would I ever boast of anything so painful to me."

"You're excused," the principal announced, wiping the incident from his mind.

Note from my passion describing this sorry event my desire for you to understand the importance of always *taking appropriate actions* to include standing up for *yourself.*

51

Korea

We were stunned to receive orders for Korea so late in Jim's career. After eighteen years of service, we had other plans than for us to send our car, our furniture, and our personal effects across another couple of oceans to a place he didn't want to be. He did everything he could to go back to Germany for another tour, but nothing worked. I was ambivalent but was pretty certain that I didn't want a fourth tour in Germany. Jeff didn't have an opinion other than to say he didn't want to move at all. (Teenage no speak?)

Because Korea is so far away, the flight is usually broken up in Tokyo. Due to our several flights back and forth I have an intimate relationship with Narita, Tokyo's airport. We have never laid foot on Japanese soil. I hope to someday.

We were exhausted when we finally arrived at Kimpo, Seoul's lackluster airport. While walking to and from the airport, we noticed for the first time the smell of the air in Korea. It was an unpleasant tinny/garlicky odor to us at first, but now just the memory of that smell makes me hungry for *Kimchi* and homesick for that time and for Korea itself.

In deference to Japan's beautiful airport, Seoul's modest, drab airport was a poor harbinger of the excitement, the adventures, the glamorous life, and the opportunities that we were about to experience on so many levels.

We were assigned a duplex near the east gate of the post. Our unit had a LR, DR, office, fireplace, two bathrooms and three bedrooms. It was partially furnished with quartermaster furniture that blended well with what we had sent from home. I had been warned to "pack light" as shopping was an amazing opportunity "over there."

Before I knew it we had moved in, received our stateside shipment, bought a "beater" (car) and I, in my own inimitable fashion, had hired a staff, having promised, once again, that I would pay their salaries from subbing.

This time, on the advice of an old friend, I hired a house boy who polished shoes, washed cars, *and black and white laundry together*, in spite of my pleas. In fair weather he did yard work. In the fall he raked leaves and in the winter he shoveled snow and ice. He also cut branches in February and put them in a vase to force a bloom, something I had never seen done. (Do this in your classrooms in the dead of winter; it's inspiring.)

I had a maid three days a week who kept the house spotless, washed windows and clothes *according to color*, started dinner, and generally made my life run smoothly. On days that I didn't have an assignment, I would hole myself in the glassed-off office and work on the columns I wrote every week for the post paper and assorted columns for the Army Times and a couple of times for the Korean Herald.

I also had a sewing lady. After she had made a model of my body, she would fashion ball gowns, dresses, suits and coats—anything I wanted created from a pattern or a mere sketch using the fabric I had purchased from the wonderland of fabric in "East Gate."

I became quite adept at the underground and could zip around Seoul easily when I didn't feel like taking a cab. Yet, I was busier as a substitute than I had ever been.

The grade school was within easy walking distance of our house, which was good news as I rarely had access to our beater. It didn't matter because I enjoyed walking and taxis were cheap and plentiful.

Teaching in Yongsan was a dream for one simple reason: parents were told that if their child misbehaved in school or did not apply him or herself appropriately *the whole family would be sent home.*

While I am not here to defend or condemn that order, I am here to tell you that the threat worked. Never before or since have I seen such positive results from parental support and universal attention to their child's school performance and overall behavior.

I taught at the grade school almost every day I was free. On Saturday's I paid my staff their weekly salary: $75.00 all together. (This was the going rate. Everything has changed since the Olympics.)

Then, I walked to the post for my Saturday hair and nails appointment: $25.00. If the staff wasn't busy, one of the beauticians would give a free back rub during the process.

Restored, I went shopping at the nearby "Chosen Gift Shop," full of treasures. Many of these treasures would make the return trip home with me.

Then, Jim and I would go downtown to enjoy a burger at "MacDonald's' and then stroll the magic street named "Itaewon" where quite literally all of your dreams could come true, to include an enormous assortment of music and videos. (NOTE: I interrupt this narrative to tell you that Mac's or Burger King Hamburger stores might look the same but almost never taste the same: They cost more and end up making you feel homesick.)

Somewhere along the line, I began getting calls to teach high school. I admit that after having subbed for eight years, I knew that I was more comfortable with little kids; but I wanted to serve where I was needed and accepted the challenge.

And then I accepted a super opportunity to teach twelfth grade sociology the rest of the year. It never occurred to me that for the last eight weeks of the school year, there would be no lesson plan, no evidence of what they had done before and, incredibly, no text book or course outline.

Add to this the unhappy fact that there was no cooperation from the unusually laconic students in the classes I was assigned or from the equally surprising laconic staff. I decided not to press; they might irritate/disappoint me. After having made gestures toward picking up any existing threads, I decided to come up with my own plan for the rest of the term. Because I loved and respected sociology, I knew that I could do it.

And, although this may not be a strictly professional observation, I was a little afraid that *someone* would come up with something boring. I knew/felt I could excel.

Since I feel as though Korea is not usually painted with the same brush of love and happy memories that I employ, I want to impress you with a simple, little known fact: Instead of landing at Kimpo, travelers now land at Incheon International Airport. Seoul-Incheon International airport (30 miles west of Seoul) is now one of the busiest international airports in the world. Since 2005 it has consistently been rated as the best airport in the world by Airports Council and the cleanest airport and best international airport by Skytrax.

The airport has a golf course, spa, private sleeping rooms, ice skating rink, a casino, indoor gardens, and a Museum of Korean Culture.

Airport authorities boast that the average departure and arrival time is nineteen and twelve minutes early, respectively. The airport also has an enviable baggage mishandling rate of 0.0001 percent, which is a number of laughable importance unless it was your suitcase that made up that percentage.

Kramer vs. Kramer

I remember Korea as having six delightfully distinct seasons, each dropping after the other like a curtain. Spring is announced with a season full of high winds, storms, rain, lightning, and roaring thunder. Power outages are the norm as we look forward to the ethereal part of spring with soft weather, gentle breezes, and trees fairly bursting with floating, fragrant blossoms.

Summer stomps in with both feet providing sizzling hot weather, deep blue skies, humidity, and temperatures best forgotten.

Then comes what we in the northwest call an "Indian summer," with more comfortable temperatures and breezes that blow spent leaves fried crisp and brown from the heat. The deep-blue skies soon will make a pretty background for these trees as autumn makes its official entrance providing the drop in temperature that paints the leaves from a fall palate to darkened winter leaves. For a couple of months we enjoyed the beauty of the leaves, the sky, and the breezes.

And then winter descends like a bully with the harshness of a fairytale stepmother cutting short your joyful excursions here and there, making them dangerous with rains, freezing temperatures, blinding snow, and insidious ice. Yet, you appreciated winter for its majesty and its uncompromising extremes.

While strolling with Jim through Itaewon one mid-spring Saturday, I was still wrestling with what to do with my sociology class. After fries and a burger that didn't taste like a Big Mac from Peoria or any other American city (they never do), I purchased a video titled *Kramer vs. Kramer*. It starred Dustin Hoffman as a "Yuppiefied" success-driven graphics artist in sales, and Meryl Streep as his unhappy, frustrated Yuppie wife.

Justin Henry, the anguished six-year old in this drama was the most appealing and believable child actor I have ever seen on film. His performance was heartbreaking.

After viewing the film a couple of times, I cherished it for the brilliance of the screenplay, direction, and the performances; but I also saw the film as a true picture of "contemporary relationships, values, needs, wants, and choices." I was reminded again that societal changes and opinions create new social mores, leaving the law, religion, and tradition in the dust. Suddenly, I knew what I would do: I would teach the rest of the term *from this video.*

We would watch it in small spurts, taking little "pop quizzes" after each viewing, participating in talk sessions about our feelings, thus far.

Then, when I thought we had seen enough for a good exchange of ideas, we would dialogue from a prepared agenda about what I saw as the key points: First, a young mom leaving her husband and child because she wanted to find herself; Second, the validity of her feelings—that she had only been someone's daughter or someone's wife or someone's mother. We would have a take-home essay test here, discussing these points.

We would talk about "Ted's" feelings. He has provided a small but comfortable New York apartment for his wife and son. Also he has worked hard and gained the respect of his colleagues and boss; in fact, he is up for a large promotion. Ted is happy. He loves his wife and his family. When confronted with "Joanna's" disappearance, he is baffled. (Another break, more writing and more discussion.)

Ted is forced to care for Billy. He loses his job over the conflicting demands on his time and concentration. He accepts help from Joanna's best friend who provides some insight into why Joanna left, yet Ted still feels in the dark. (Break/writing/dialogue.)

Joanna gets her act together admitting that she felt like a bad mother before, but now she has a better grip on herself after seeking psychiatric help and finding a good job. Now, she wants full custody of "her son." (Break: writing and heady discussion.)

The legal ramifications were a good source of study and discussion too. We discussed the trial and the arguments each side presented. We wrote about and discussed the judge's decision to give Joanna full custody and her unexpected decision to relinquish her hard-won victory seeing how connected Ted and her son have become in her absence. At this point I designed a formal test to measure each student's perceptions and grasp of the important points presented. The results were impressive.

The excitement was there in each period, and I couldn't wait to get to school as we yearned to defend our various positions and strike down those in opposition.

And then, someone stole the video.

To my astonishment we didn't need it anymore. Our hour together was alive with vivid explorations and lively discussions. Although I didn't think of it then, we could have done role playing; we could have done reversals where a male played Joanna and a female played Ted. We could have gone on for more time. We had struck a rich vein.

What we did together lasts in my memory as good. I think that I planted the basic fact that looking through a "sociological lens," *that right or wrong is based on where you live and, further, right or wrong depends on when and where you were born.*

There are thousands of movies that would make a good study from many angles, not just sociology but many disciplines. *The Three Faces of Eve* would work well for psychology, *The Great Gatsby* for literature or film (the Robert Redford film, please). Then for the Gifted student there is *Shine*. For Special Ed and Handicapped, *My Left Foot*; cooking, *Julia vs. Julia*.

Any class that deals with *cause and effect,* a major factor in training young people to live productively, accepting themselves, and making good choices is a good approach. When it's all said and done, cause and effect is all there is.

In my estimation, from the first time a student enters our system, each day should deal with CAUSE AND EFFECT in class work, reading, math, games, seatwork, art, and in physical education, but especially in their interaction with their teachers and their peers.

Why not stress from the earliest time we have our students that their choices determine their destination: That cause and effect is all. We can do this. We must do this.

This kind of training should not offend any religious or non-religious group. This outlook is simply good common sense, which does not appear to be very common today.

The last chapter in this book will briefly explore this subject further with some concrete suggestions.

A Summer "Thrillogy"

That summer the three of us took a dream vacation partially funded by my substitute teaching.

As soon as school was out, we (Jeff, Jim and I) booked a special tour through Thai Air. Our first destination was Bangkok, Thailand, where we had lived twelve years ago.

In those days, flying was a real treat. We were treated like first-class passengers receiving fresh orchids, free drinks, and an appealing meal during each of the three legs of our week-long trip.

Although Jeff was only three during our assignment in Bangkok, he remembered isolated events, especially when we drove by our villa. Of course it was hot in Bangkok and the traffic was crazy, but we enjoyed the tours and the fabulous meals from familiar restaurants. I was overwhelmed at seeing the exotic city I never dreamed I would see again. I bought some brass rubbings to remember the event; in fact I bought twenty-five rubbings— rice paper embossed with Thai figures costing the equivalent of a quarter each.

Our second stop was Kuala Lumpur, a new visit for us and much less hectic than Bangkok, yet full of wonderful sights, food, and shopping opportunities. My usually frugal husband, who "doesn't want to lug heavy souvenirs around," bought not one but two extremely heavy, extremely old irons that were designed to be filled with hot coals. I chuckle to myself each time I dust the unwieldy brass and the pewter *object d' art.*

Our last stop was the island of Singapore. Whenever I thought of Singapore I thought of a place of romance, mystery, and Oriental intrigue. I thought of many cultures living in close quarters and sailors who worked at what was once the busiest port in the world, roaming the city causing excitement and mayhem.

Strangely, an effort has been in effect to "sanitize" Singapore with rules and regulations. The most drastic measure was to clear away the shanty towns, placing poor people into bland, government apartments, effectively wiping away the ethnicity and the charm that Singapore once held for romantics like me. The charm of "Raffles" was still there—an ancient open-air bar with birds flying around at will, probably as they did when Somerset Maugham was there, gathering fodder for one of his charming stories.

We were tired at the end of our week visiting Bangkok, Kuala Lumpur, the Straights of Malacca, and Singapore. It was late June and very hot in all three cities because they are so close to the equator. You might think that the natives who endure this kind of heat would get used to it, but after having "live-in-staff," I can tell you that they do not. There was as much griping and sniveling from their quarters over the heat as from ours. People are people.

It was a good thing that we had taken this marvelous trip and stored so many happy memories as the next summer I would accept a job full of back-breaking, mind-boggling effort and challenges, some with frightening and dangerous possibilities.

Summer Hire

Beginning with the first Monday of the second week in June, I would take a cab across town to another army post, simply referred to as "Embassy." There was a fancy club on post designed for the Embassy staff's use, but not exclusively. We dined there many times.

Within the confines of the post was a school where, with the help of an aide, I would teach two classes each day of fifteen three-year olds. Additionally, twice a week, each class, my PE, and I would go to a swimming pool.

Looking at that paragraph, I see how often it is possible to innocently outline a teaching situation that is rife with opportunities for hardship and untold disaster.

The first day of school I appeared in a dress I designed and my sewing lady put together so well that I had her make another from different fabrics. Close your eyes and imagine Julie Andrews from the *Sound of Music* wearing a Bavarian dress of a tiny Tyrolean print with an apron in another color. Of necessity, due to the intense heat in our classroom and the exertion of physically handling thirty little bodies, my dresses were sleeveless. Part of this intense exertion was due to the fact that virtually none of our three year-olds wanted to be at school. (The PE and the teacher felt the same way, initially.)

For the first two weeks, everyone cried, even my youthful Korean aide. I was the only adult around, if you don't count the Korean grandmothers who lurked outside the building, waving in at the little ones they had managed to spoil so effectively.

Persistence alone propelled me to gather the suffering mass into something resembling a circle; and with puppets, games, songs, and stories, little by little the students and the aide decided to take an interest in what our pre-school class had to offer.

This was a good thing as after the first two weeks that little caveat called *taking the children swimming on Tuesdays and Thursday* was to become a reality.

Because I try to maintain a positive attitude, I envisioned lining up our babies (by now I recognized that they were little more than that) and guiding them to a nearby building where a sparkling little pool of warm, blue water would beckon them to enter.

Pool day arrived and with it the misery of changing fifteen fat little bodies into bathing suits being careful, all the while, to keep their clothes separate from those of the other squirming little fat bodies who now needed to stuff their fat little feet into flip flops.

NOTE: The job of stuffing a little piggy foot into a flip flop is one thing but to keep it on is quite another.

Needless to say there was more crying with my aide, Ms. Din, leading the pack. Through her tears, she resolutely helped me line up our little ones and check for:

- ✓ Bathing suits on properly, i.e. front-first. Check!
- ✓ Flip-flops on the "right feet" (eventually, we would give up on this one). Check!
- ✓ Towel appropriately draped or neatly folded. Check!
- ✓ School clothes folded in their "cubbies" (cupboards). Check!

The next step was figuratively and physically a big one. My visions of a short walk on post to a friendly pool were dashed when an enormous army green bus pulled up to transport our class to "THE POOL."

Korean drivers are to be congratulated. I thought Bangkok traffic was terrible and that Thai drivers, male/female, were crazy; but they don't hold a candle to Korean drivers.

But that was down the line. The first concern was to lift each little one up the deep stairs, catching their towel and at least one "flip" in the process. I took the bottom step and Ms. Din was the receiver of the child and the other "flop." (I honestly didn't want to see what happened after they entered the bus.) By the time I climbed the stairs, the children had found a place to sit, and I attempted to stress that "since there are no seatbelts, you will have to hold on." (I didn't tell them what to hold on to because I didn't know what their little arms could grasp to keep them safe, if indeed safety was even a remote possibility.

With the first lurch of the bus and the first slam of the brakes, I envisioned cracked teeth, concussions, and cut lips. Instead, like little butterballs, my babies slithered out of their seats and on to the floor and rolled down the aisle. They and we soon took this in stride. Each slither required Ms. Din or me to reseat them while rumbling through the heavy traffic, the heat, and the smell of cheap gas.

And then I saw it! *My* mink coat.

Just as I returned after another rescue mission I noticed that we were on Itaewon, "my magic street." In fact, we were almost at Jindo, the fur and leather shop I had visited recently. I had tried on a full-length black mink coat with a small stand-up collar. The design was clean, simple, and comfortable.

There it was, in the window for me to see on each trip to the swimming pool!

Suddenly, I knew I had to have it and that *if* I had this vision in my mind, I could get through this summer no matter what it brought. But that was before disaster hit.

Earning a Mink Coat
the Hard Way

Because I am an optimist with pragmatic overtones, I recognized that to enjoy my mink coat I would not only have to get through my summer teaching three-year-olds but so would they. How could I wear a coat remembering any kind of casualty during my time as their teacher? (I cannot bear to revisit some of the worries that tortured me.)

But never could I have imagined that the worst risk to my students would not be from anything I or Ms. Din did or did not do, nor did it lie in the snarl of Korea traffic or from slithering out of a seat onto the floor of an army bus, or even the danger of falling in the deep end of an enormous swimming pool. No, the insidious attack would be in the warm and cozy classroom Ms. Din and I had so lovingly assembled for our little ones.

Near Embassy Post was a city college where, as in other countries, young people feel free to revolt for various reasons. It escapes my mind what they were revolting about or against as they tear-gassed our school and seemingly our classroom in particular. All I know is that without any warning, we felt a stinging in our eyes and throat and found it hard to breathe or speak.

Our children, not knowing any better, sucked in more poisonous air by crying and rubbing their eyes. Having never been subjected to a tear gas attack, I had no antidote to what I saw going on. There was no way to calm the children because I couldn't speak. All I could think to do was to moisten paper towels that the children could use to breathe through to ease the sting in their eyes and throats.

Of course the ever-present Korean grandmothers *(Halmonis)* outside our windows were frantic too and banged on the windows to get their grandchildren's attention.

We were gassed three times; and while it never got easier, we learned to deal with it reminiscent of the way the Brits handled air raids, I suppose.

It pleases me to say that that summer lingers in my mind as a happy and injury-free eight weeks and that my beautiful mink coat still hangs proudly in our coat closet.

We have moved several times since Korea and I have lost track of my "Julie Andrews" dresses, but I know they are somewhere.

I never throw a happy memory away, especially one so hard fought and so soundly won.

What to Do When You Don't Know What to Do
(Part 3)

A True-Life 4th Grade Challenge

"Ms. Knight?

"Yes, Coltin."

"Damon spit in your thermos this morning."

"Thank you. That's very helpful information."

In Chapter Three discussing what to do on your first day of subbing, I casually mentioned that you should secure your thermos. I didn't have the heart to tell you why, just then, as I wanted you to feel more sure of yourself in the classroom before I shared some of the seamier sides of classroom experiences.

What to do? Since it was dismissal time and the teacher was returning the next day, I decided not to confront Damon. I elected to stay calm and do nothing until I discovered a good course of action. (I was doing well, so far, in not over-reacting.)

In the singular loveliness of an empty classroom, the air still charged from the students' energy slowly dissipates as you turn on your Boom Box, put on your slippers, and write a brief but professionally worded note to Damon. You glance at the seating chart, just to make sure it was his seat, and leave your note encased in red colored paper where he can't fail to find it. Then you empty your thermos into the classroom sink, rinse it, stow it, take a swig from your refillable bottle of mouth-wash from your TK, and gargle and spit into the sink.

Done and done.

Turning the Tides in Grades 4–6

These grades can be especially challenging as the students are becoming more complex and so is their course of study: "Let's diagram a sentence… Bueller… anyone?"

The first step when you see your students' eyes glazing over or their rapt lack of attention during your fascinating presentation on multiplying fractions is to pull out your *Boom Box* and ask them to stand and do "in-place" exercises. (Use these for 1–6.) Or, stay seated and do deep-breathing exercises also to music (grades 3–12). These breaks show that you, as a teacher, understand when they feel bored or overwhelmed with a difficult lesson. You are letting them know that you understand their restlessness, and rather than punish them you are teaching them some relaxation techniques that they might use forever. Of course, the old standby is to erase the board and draw a Hangman Noose. This is usually a pleasant diversion for class and teacher alike. Or, have a "Go To" story you've carefully selected for each age group. Invite them to put their heads down and listen to you read.

This age group also responds well to "free time" coupons. Pull out some interesting diversions from your TK or leave those you think you can trust to their own devices.

Handling Bad Situations: Pre-K–K

Even if you don't have a lesson plan, it's easy, after you've taught awhile to know what to do with Pre K–K. After the bell has rung, take roll while they are in their seats, and do the "Pledge of Allegiance." Then ask your little ones to gather around you for "circle." Normally, there will be a rocking chair on a rug indicating the "circle" area. There, you will introduce yourself, reassuring them that their teacher will likely "be back tomorrow, happy to see you, and *glad that I was able to say we had a fine day together.*" (A thinly veiled threat?) You will talk about your day, play a game, or sing a song or two.

The rest of the day, or half day for little ones, deals with workbooks, language arts and math exercises, juice and cracker break, playtime, recess, songs, and a story.

Normally, this full schedule keeps them busy enough to occupy even the most over-active child. But what if it doesn't?

1. If things are deteriorating, often during play time, dim the lights; wait for quiet.

2. Lower your voice and in a near whisper say that they need to be quieter.

3. Leave the lights off and remind them that "we need to be considerate of one another." Shana, do you know what "considerate" means? Keep asking for the best answer. (Often teachers, inadvertently, use words their students do not understand.)

4. Then say, "Sometimes it's difficult to know when you're playing too hard or too loud so I will sing a little song to remind you." (Hum a few bars of a "reminder song.")

5. Turn the lights back on to resume their normal activity but if they become boisterous again and do not respond to your reminder song, call them back into circle and you and your hand puppet discuss what kinds of behavior they need to modify.

It isn't hard to identify an over-active child. During student teaching I was tasked with calling the mother of such a child to discuss the situation. The mother agreed that he was hyper and that his favorite thing to do at home was to pull out the silverware drawer.

"He's supposed to be on Ritalin but I couldn't bear the thought."

As a mother I understood; as a teacher, not so much.

For Grades 1–3

Opportunities for chaos abound even at this age.

It used to be that grades 1–3 were years of gentleness, and trust. Yet it seems that kids lose their innocence and their sense of wonder earlier each year. Although it's natural to wonder why and feel sad, the fact is that teachers need to deal with what is.

And, right now you have a problem. What to do?

It is imperative that students have their names on their desk (or on their person) so you can call on them. It is also important that you take roll and make sure that the names match the seating chart you should have. If the class is full there is no problem, but absenteeism is. In fact truancy is a bigger problem than ever before.

Now, there is turmoil or a disturbance: Let's say a fist fight between two students, not necessarily boys. (Do not touch them or try to separate them.)

First, grab some seatwork to hand out. Announce to the class that there will be prizes for the best job. "Class, I know that Rachel and Sheena are having a problem, but you don't have to be part of it. I am handing out a puzzle for you to solve. The first three students to get it right will win a prize. (The fight is still going on, but what you are doing will draw the attention away from a fight that might even resolve itself as the rest of the class turns their attention to an interesting hand-out and the promise of "prizes.")

Focus on the fight and when there seems to be a break, ask the pugilists to sit. Tell them that after they have cooled down they will have some special seat work, and that on completion you have a special surprise for them. (Some "I Chilled-Out" water?)

This is an extreme measure to defuse an extreme situation. Try dimming the light, going to the board and simply drawing the "Hangman's Noose" to their attention.

(Hangman is adaptable to almost any age group.) Here's how: After drawing the frame, turn and face the class, waiting for their attention. When you have it, turn back to the board and draw lines for each letter in the word you choose. I begin the game with an easy word for their level; and later, if they are interested in playing, I ask them to take a piece of paper and submit a word they think would be tricky. (In upper grades you can use words like "Czechoslovakia," or "onyx," "sphinx," "chrysanthemum," or "Tyrolean," or "gypsy." (Words with consonants close together provide a challenge.) Often, just an abrupt change of pace, like Hangman, defuses the situation and the class is ready to return to their work refreshed.

Another easy defuser is "Secret." Even if the class is out of sorts—they are too warm, cold, bored or upset for their own reasons—you can effectively turn this around.

Ask if they have played "Secret" before. Divide the class in half indicating the "last person" on each side.

Explain that you are going to whisper a sentence to the first person in the row nearest the window and the same sentence to the first person nearest the door. They are to quietly whisper the sentence to the person behind them and so on until the last person receives the message, which they will write down. (Or tell you.) When both sides are finished ask the last persons to stand and tell the class what they heard. MAKE IT CLEAR THAT TALKING DURING THE GAME DISQUALIFIES YOUR TEAM. Have the person who finished first read their message and then the second person. Then, you read the message you had sent to each side. (It's almost never the same.) How messages get distorted is a life-lesson in itself and, incidentally, a lot of fun.

Another easy game to "clear the air in a hurry" is "Button, Button." (You can use a piece of chalk or any "safe" item.) Choose someone to go to each student and "pretend" to slide the object into their hands. Offer a prize to the person(s) who correctly identifies who has the object. This game teaches concentration and attention to detail and it's fun! Again, caution there is to be no talking or "coaching" your teammates.

Sometimes you need a combination of stress-breakers. The easiest way to start is with deep-breathing exercises or standing-in-place exercises. Once the oxygen has been replaced, students feel better and are ready to cooperate either with a game, a contest, or remarkably, any work you wish for them to complete.

Some groups respond well to "free time." If you feel you have such a group, play something soothing on your *Boom Box* and savor the almost palatable good feeling in the air of a classroom in harmony.

Now, go back over your lesson plan and make certain that you have covered everything. This is why you are here. This would also be a good time to count hand-in work against your roster. Some students ignore the act of actually *handing in their work.* They often do not expect a substitute to catch their omission.

Perhaps they never had a sub quite like you before?

Right on!

Before we launch into the next chapter I would like to share a hint that makes dealing with husbands, children, and octogenarians a lot easier.

When you want to call attention to an object or a direction, say something like, "Look at Ms. Knight's finger." Then, with or without a drum roll, simply point to the object you desire your subject/subjects to observe. "See, honey, the toaster's over there," or "See class, the winners in the spelling tests are mounted back there," or "Gramma, I put your jammies over here." Trust me on this one: introduce your "pointy-finger, often."

The Butterfly Teacher

It was Veteran's Day when I accepted a job in a school I did not know. It was clear that the school was in a poor neighborhood, but the building was attractive and well maintained. Two third grades, my class and another, were located away from the rest of the school, both physically and in every other way, as I would find.

The fifteen students in my class were not referred to as Special Ed students; and truthfully not all of them presented special problems, yet I knew something was wrong.

First, it is unusual to have a class that small. Also, it was only the second time a principal escorted me to a classroom and the second time a principal seemed to want to give me tips on how to get through the day. He was like a salesperson selling a used car.

(A clunker?)

My last clue would appear as I attempted to conduct the class according to the teacher's lesson plans. Something wasn't right; the atmosphere was discordant.

At this point I had subbed for thirteen years; and in a case like this, where I could feel the disharmony, see the brokenness in the faces of some of the students, and feel it in their behavior, I knew we were in trouble.

As a sub I was usually inspired to "fix things," to turn things around and enjoy our day: *day* being the key word. I didn't *have* to stay in a situation I found uncomfortable.

In spite of my misgivings, I accepted, when I was asked back, escorted again by the principal who heaped praise on me for the "splendid job I had done." He asked me to fill out the week, still not letting me know that the regular teacher, Ms. Gerhardt, was out on maternity leave and that no one was standing in line to take over her class. (If I had known this I would have found this unusual too. Usually, pregnant teachers hand pick or at least suggest their long-term subs to insure a smooth transition on their return.)

By this time we had retired from the army, *over my dead body*, and were living in Steilacoom, Washington. I hadn't been ready to retire as we had received word that Japan might be our next assignment. I was excited about this possibility but Jim was not. And there was Jeff to think about. He was about to begin school either at West Point, if he got an appointment, or at the University of Washington in Seattle.

To state that there was a lot of tension and drama going on in our lives would be a disservice to tension and drama. Stated bluntly, we needed more money. Returning to civilian life had turned out to be more expensive than we had expected. Jim had applied in many different areas for work but was deemed "over-qualified," again and again.

He had tried subbing and found it a bad fit. This statement is also something of an insult to "bad fits." (See chapter three.) He gave up wanting to teach full-time but secretly hoped I would find a full-time teaching position that appealed to me.

I felt as though a noose was slowly descending down around my neck as I struggled to teach this group of super-needy kids. As the week wore on, I saw that they were sucking the life out of me; yet they needed me to be strong, skillful, patient, and understanding all day, everyday. I needed to teach, nurture, encourage, and counsel.

On one hand I wanted to do a good job: to turn the insolent behavior of three of the boys around; to inspire a couple of them to do their best on their seatwork or at least to *do something*; to calm the classroom into a cohesive unit to "make things nice" for the three immaculately groomed, docile little girls who did everything I asked them to do.

And then there was the small, wiry class clown and his able assistants. His brand of merriment would have made you laugh had you not been me, his teacher.

And then there was Delaney, the most mysterious student of all. She was nearly as tall as I and at least twice as smart. She could read on a tenth or twelfth grade level and, when she felt like it, could have conducted the class with her adroit knowledge of human nature and her skill at manipulation. That was what was creepy about this woman-child: she *seemed to have super-human powers and gifts far beyond her year group. Why was she in this class? What was her story?*

The week finally came to a close, and although I had not dazzled anyone after the first day, the principal saw that I was still standing and set the noose firmly in place asking me to fill in until Ms. Gerhardt returned from her maternity leave. I begged the weekend to think about the offer of filling in for the badly missed (by all) Ms. Gerhardt.

Everything inside me knew I shouldn't take this class from "The Twilight Zone." It wasn't that I was being ungenerous. I just knew that we would end up breaking each other's hearts. I clung to the term, "fill-in." In my heart I knew I was a "Butterfly teacher" going lightly here and there. I was not a "heavy-lifter." I was not the mother robin who wanted to deal with a nest of needy birds whose beaks were open wide expecting me to provide juicy worm after worm.

Yet, I accepted the job and prayed and worried.

I am embarrassed to say, we needed the money.

This is so often the reason for bad decisions.

Shoulda, Oughta, Coulda

You would think that handling ten mildly disturbed children out of a class of fifteen would be possible. It should have been, but the constant battle I waged just keeping students occupied and in their seats was taking a toll on *me*. I also found it difficult to present a lesson that would reach the most indifferent students, the students who had learning disabilities, the normal girls, and Delaney who could have taught us all.

My confidence was shaken. Anxiety that I had conquered long ago surfaced and threatened to overwhelm me again. I was waging a war to subdue my own anxiety as I struggled to teach a class and address their emotional challenges as well as mine own.

I consoled myself with the fact that soon Ms Gerhardt would return. How much longer would she be out? I've taught six weeks already. Shouldn't that be long enough? No definitive answer was forthcoming and I didn't push, fearing the worst.

My mind has blocked out the day I was told that Ms. Gerhardt wasn't returning. Looking back, I should have insisted on a contract. I imagine I would still have accepted the challenge to finish the year thinking that there would be some breakthrough, that I would find the combination to ease the class full of unique individuals into a cohesive unit, helping one another instead of remaining solitary units of misery and confrontation and mediocre performances.

In deference to my time in Korea, where the parents were forced to be involved in their children's scholastic lives, these kids were often woefully neglected, or "raising themselves," as the principal so often said. Some of my kids fit that bill and left me feeling inadequate. I was also surprised at the weekly teacher's meetings at the amount of effort we were expected to exert outside the classroom, mostly money raisers or auctions.

A most astonishing event that year was the surprise appearance of Maya Angelou. My class entered the auditorium quietly and sat there in stillness. Every class and each student assembled seemed totally unimpressed with the black poet's performance. I was disappointed for them and for her. She, like I, hadn't reached these kids. It was palpable.

And then, after occasional nights of restlessness, I developed severe insomnia. The stress I endured during the day robbed me of the sleep I needed to do a good job and face another day. I took the brave, drastic, and expensive move to find a psychiatrist to help me. I felt as though I owed this effort not only to myself but to my students.

I was given brief conversations and modest amounts of medication. It was up to me to decide if I wanted to sleep or to *make it through the day.*

The doctor shared with me the fact that many of his stressed-out patients were teachers. (I should have shared with him that I knew why and that I needed more meds.)

Let's stop right here to see what I did do and what I "shoulda" done in addition to seeking help from a less-than-helpful psychiatrist to make that year a success:

1. I should have asked to contact Ms. Gerhardt to ask her for hints and insight on handling her class and for background on some of the more problematical students.

2. Looked for a mentor. The principal directed me to find one and I did, in name only. It appeared to me that each teacher had her own brand of misery and didn't need mine.

3. I should have worked with the school counselor. He was already seeing several of my students. It was he who talked to me about Jahel, whose poor performance baffled us.

Jahel was handsome, well nourished, and beautifully groomed in deference to many of the other students. His mom was attractive, smart, and interested in her under-achieving son.

"What is wrong?" I pleaded with the counselor. "Why won't Jahel cooperate with me?" His answer stunned and wounded me.

"Jahel doesn't *want* to please you."

I should have dug deeper for help handling Jahel and the other students he worked with. But I was embarrassed and didn't want to know if more students felt like Jahel.

When we were in Korea, I heard a Chinese General say something I never forgot: "All things end, even bad things." I used to quote that until I realized it isn't true. As in the case of a severe handicap or in an abusive relationship the "badness" does not end. My bad year seemingly had no end, and the problems I saw in so many of my students were likely to get only worse and I felt inadequate to help them.

1. Peer pressure can be effective. I should have used Delaney as a helper. I resisted doing this because she was so bossy and, because with good reason, I didn't trust her. Now, I see that I might have harnessed her talents to help me in my own overload and made her feel better about herself, too.

2. I should have talked with my teacher friends who had supported me before.

3. I should have used Jim in another way other than correcting math papers. I needed to see what the kids weren't getting. Just looking at their scores wasn't enough. He might have come in from time to time as a "guest speaker" or dressed

up like an army Colonel to talk about the military the same way policemen appear in classrooms. Or just made little visits to cheer me on and or help with my sagging morale with a Burger King.

And then a fragile miracle happened. Something that united my troubled little class in a way that I hope they remember as much as I do.

Hope

Evie, Jim's stepmother, had been a teacher for many years. She saw my angst during the school year but said little until she gave me a hint that turned things around. Evie was a lady who wouldn't share her recipes, but, in the end, she saved my bacon.

One evening while we were enjoying her secret recipe for lasagna, she casually tossed me a catalog she had saved full of science projects.

By now I fully accepted the fact that school districts never had enough money and that every teacher, with a soul, used their own money to buy things to enrich their day.

With this thought in mind I ordered a "Butterfly Kit" at Evie's suggestion.

As any teacher would, I talked about this kit (read: beat the subject to death) in an attempt to inculcate a little excitement and unity into our last couple of months of misery. I felt a gentle undercurrent of interest.

When the kit arrived I explained everything I could about the various stages a butterfly goes through: "egg, larva (caterpillar), pupa, and adult. As we watched this metamorphoses I felt their curiosity and a little encouraging unity over our butterfly.

Then it died. Or, let us say it stopped "metamorphosizing" out of the pupa stage. And so we talked a little about death. Neither I nor my students were comfortable with that subject. However, Delaney seemed to know a lot about it which was a huge help.

It was at this time that I began receiving frequent phone calls from Delaney's new stepmother. Together, we puzzled over her behavior and tried to find a strategy to help what we knew to be an over-bearing, manipulative, driven, terribly troubled, scary girl.

Although I didn't have much faith in the project, I reordered the butterfly kit, hoping it would make it this time and produce a gorgeous yellow and black specimen—something good that we would associate with our time together. Now we were completely united in this project; I discovered that people unite over tragedy as well as joy.

All during the dreary early spring, I continued to suffer from insomnia and to receive calls from Delaney's mom as we continued to compare notes about her behavior and how best to understand it. Somewhere along the line I came up with a theory I could not share with anyone except the school counselor. I felt uncomfortable doing this, at that time, but later I would regret my inaction with all of my heart.

Delaney was attractive: her advanced physical and mental maturity, her reading and math skills appropriate to an eighth grader, her mood swings, her outbursts, her lies, her flares of temper, her manipulative personality, her lack of close friends, except for little kids, suggested to me that Delaney had been or was being sexually abused.

The new kit arrived. We had already drilled ourselves blue in the face on the four stages of a butterfly's life. Now we constructed a net "house" with branches inside for the eventual attachment in the pupa stage.

This time the interest was even more intense than before. We were more united than ever. Enthusiastically, I designed the remaining weeks around our butterfly. We made butterfly kites and 3-D butterflies, ate butterfly cookies, made caterpillars pictures, and made caterpillars out of cotton balls and phony fur. We read and wrote stories about butterflies, sang butterfly songs, wore butterfly wings, danced butterfly dances. Our math was based on caterpillar and butterfly facts. Geography was all about butterfly regions.

We discussed and looked at pictures of the butterfly museum in downtown Seattle. As united as we were becoming, even if there had been enough money in the budget, which there was not, I wouldn't have wanted to escort my gang to a big city museum, anywhere.

When it was pretty clear that we were going to actually see our butterfly evolve we had a contest to name her. It was an exciting event, and I thought the winning name was perfect. We named our soon-to-be-butterfly "Hope."

To properly appreciate what transpired you need to see a copy of the old classic "The Music Man." To us, when she finally came to life and flew around, she was the most beautiful creature ever born. To someone unlucky enough not to be in Ms. Knight's third grade, Hope was more moth than a Monarch. Incredible as it sounds, we let her out for long stretches and handled her so gently that she didn't mind being enclosed again.

Now, as time was dwindling down, we talked about letting go of someone you can't keep. We talked about separation, loss, and *doing the right thing.*

We were united in our sorrow the last full day of school as, after the last bell, we went out on the porch and let her fly away. There were tears, but the thought of summer vacation was an appealing anecdote for each of us, especially for me.

With a heavy heart I unlocked the door of our classroom the next morning. We would share a last half day together knowing that the light was gone from our classroom.

But what did I see when I opened the door? I saw Hope flying around our room.

And so did even the most damaged of my struggling little ones. No one could explain or guess how it happened. It didn't matter because Hope was back for each of us.

Appendix 1
The Art of Defusing

Carolyn's Story

I need to give a nod to one of my teacher friends who shared her teaching story with me for this book. Carolyn, an old friend and an army wife, is married to a former army helicopter pilot with harrowing Vietnam experiences. Here's her own harrowing story:

"Carolyn, do you have something you'd like to add to my book on subbing?"

"You bet I do," she answered, not slowing down to take a breath. "It was the summer I graduated, shortly before we got married.

"I lived in Portland and accepted a third-grade assignment. The class was rowdy and disrespectful, to say the least. I gave 'em a lot of chances to cool down but they just ignored me.

"There was this one kid who really tested the waters, and I zeroed in on him thinking if I could coral him that I'd encourage (read scare) the rest of the class."

"What happened?" I asked, fearing the answer, based my own experiences.

"He ignored me... but I pursued him. I did everything I knew to get him to sit down but he wouldn't. He jumped out of the window instead."

"How'd that go?"

"Not so well. Our classroom was on the third floor and he broke his beg."

"Did they fire you?"

83

"No, they hired me to sit all day, every day overseeing third grade 'detention.' I worked there till the end of the year. I never had a bit of trouble."

That is one style of defusing, but there are others.

The Fine Art of Defusing

My thirty-pound dictionary is usually super wordy when all I need is a quick fix. But this time, when I could have used something lofty, I am left with this:

Defuse: "1. *to remove the fuse from a bomb, or the like,* 2. *to render harmless.*"

I am okay with this explanation. If you have ever seen an eight-grader (or the like) about to explode, you would see the similarity. And if you ever rendered him/her harmless by simply drawing a "Hangman Noose" on the board or slipped them some interesting seatwork, you'd get it.

The hard part about diverting the time bomb (so you can remove the fuse) is that the rest of the class often sees your efforts as "coddling" bad behavior. They might want to be given what they see as a "privilege" for themselves: A free pass, seatwork and the like. If that is the case, offer it to them *as soon as they have finished their assigned work.*

"Why doesn't Diante have to do the assignment?"
"She does. She is responsible to turn in her work, tomorrow."
"Why doesn't she have to do it now?"
"Because I have another special assignment for her."
"What's that?"
"It's something between the two of us."
"That's not fair."
"Okay. Do you want to fill out a special questionnaire too? As

soon as you have finished what the teacher asked us to do, it's yours." (Checkmate)

Diagnostic Questionnaire for Grades 3–12

Fill out this questionnaire according to directions and you will have a choice of a reward for a job well done. Answer in full sentences. You may exceed the number of sentences required. You have this period to complete at least half of the questionnaire. Read the questions carefully and then select the questions you want to answer as completely as you can. (Spelling is not important on this quiz.)

1. Am I having a bad day? If so, do I know why? (Two full sentences)
2. What can I do to fix it? (One sentence)
3. If I was the teacher what would I tell my teacher to do right now? (Two sentences)
4. What time did I go to sleep last night? (One full sentence)
5. Did I eat breakfast this morning? (One sentence including what you ate.)
6. Most of the time I like school or do not like school? Why? (Five sentences)
7. What do I look for in a friend? (One sentence)
8. What do I not like in a friend? (One sentence)
9. When am I the happiest? (Two sentences)
10. What makes me unhappy? (List ten things)
11. How can I get happier? (Three sentences)
12. How can I avoid feeling sad? (Three sentences)
13. How can I avoid feeling angry? Who can I talk to? (Two sentences)

14. What are my favorite TV programs? Movies? DVDs, CDs, Video Games?

15. What is my favorite sport to play? To watch?

16. Who (alive or dead; male or female) inspires me? Why? (Three sentences)

17. What are my plans for the future? (Two sentences)

18. What can I do to make any dreams I have come true? (Three sentences)

19. What are my ideas of a better world? (Two sentences)

20. What is something no one knows about me? (One sentence)

How to Defuse a Bad Situation
Grades Pre-K-1

Because names are a crucial tool to run a smooth classroom at Pre K–K, I pack "sticky" name tags in my TK, just in case.

Working with good defusing techniques, when a situation occurs in a classroom or when the general atmosphere is tense and unproductive, have the students stand and choose from the following:

1. Do some deep breathing exercises, which you will demonstrate.

2. Stretches: "Can you reach the ceiling standing on tippy toes?"

3. Do some seat games.

4. Sing a clapping song.

If the tense situation involves a child who is crying and needs your attention, then revert to seatwork. Pass it out to students and tend to the crying child, one-on-one. Note: There are many fine websites that have black line masters, some for a minimal yearly fee.

Diverting seat work could be art work and puzzles or age-appropriate word or math games. After you have settled the upset child, you might continue the "healing process" with teacher-generated games or songs. If the child is still upset, ask permission to hold them or seat them close as you direct teacher-generated activities or read a story.

Another technique to defuse a tense situation is to call "circle" again. Use your hand puppet to talk about whatever behavior or classroom rules have been broken. Keep it light and speak in a soothing manner, making eye contact with each of your students.

While they are gathered together, you might play a guessing game: "I am thinking of someone in our circle who is wearing a red and blue shirt." This game is a great diversion technique as well as a vocabulary enhancement opportunity. The bottom line is that the air is cleared of tension so you can get on with the day with everyone feeling good.

Allow them to resume their activities if they have control of themselves, but dismiss them one by one from circle: "I see that London is ready for play time. London, you may get up and slowly go to the play area. "Hmm, I wonder who will be the next one to be sitting ever so quietly with their hands to themselves?"

When everyone is back on track, you might want to play something cheerful on your Boom Box. Carly Simon's "Itsy Bitsy Spider" usually makes everyone feel good.

How to Defuse a Bad Situation
Grades 1–3

Come into classes at these levels with your TK full of "prizes:" (See Appendix 2.) *These kids will work for prizes.* (It is a small price to pay for the opportunity to actually teach.)

Crisis: Often, you don't have time to *know who did what to whom*. For sure there is usually enough blame to go around in a one-on-one confrontation. What to do? Seat one child facing the left side of the board in the front of the room and another on the right side. Settle the class with an assignment or seatwork. Draw your chair up beside the first child. (This is better than hovering over them, less menacing, and easier on your back.)

Quietly ask him/her what happened. Allow the child to return to his seat and the seatwork. If the infraction had been serious (biting, punching, hitting) or if they are still upset, have the child put his/her head on their desk as you proceed to the second child.

Next, cover the lesson plans, promising a small prize "For your patience while Kennedy, Paris, and I work through our problems."

Then bring the two students together. Have a set of stickers or some other small reward visible that you are prepared to give to them if they resolve their problems *and* apologize to each other. Allow them to choose from the rewards you lay out while you walk around the class putting stickers or other small prizes on their desks for "'staying on-task' while Kennedy, Paris, and I talked together." There are no losers with little kids, or as a teacher friend once said, "There are only second, third, fourth, fifth, sixth… winners."

How to Defuse Problems
Grades 4–6

It's not so much that you are bribing your students to behave, although I feel that approval and success are bribes in and of themselves. You just have to be a bit more sophisticated with this age group and broaden your rewards from stickers to include free-time vouchers. Who doesn't want to do "what they want to do?" Allowing them to spend time looking through the selected magazines and comic books you have brought, or doing any reasonable thing *they* want to do, relieves you of having to select a reward.

But how do you introduce prizes to induce calm when chaos has broken out in class and you, as a sub, don't know these kids well enough to quickly find a solution?

It all begins with your introductions. After the class has assembled, you've taken careful roll, done the flag salute, and introduced yourself, you need to set the perimeters."

What perimeters?

"Your teacher has left a very clear lesson plan and if we accomplish this by 1:30 this afternoon, I have an interesting project that I think you will like. How well we cooperate will let me know how much you are 'into' a project that other kids have liked."

You have put the onus on them. More than that, you have suggested that the class *needs to work together* to earn the prize. When a class is working together, they monitor themselves and others; peer pressure is often very effective and something beautiful to see.

See Appendix 2 for "neat" projects and ideas for inexpensive rewards.

So, the perimeters are set but a couple of students decide that they don't want to cooperate; they are rude and disruptive. If they continue to cause a commotion, put a chair facing the board for each offender. Speak to them separately. When they have cooled off, hand them the diagnostic questionnaire (p. 85) to be filled out at their desks. If they miss an assignment, make it home work. If they cooperate, let them join in on "the project." It is important to show forgiveness and clear the air of any hostility.

How to Defuse Problems
Grades 6–8

These students are often in your class for only an hour at a time. This is good news and bad news. The bad news is that you don't have a chance to bond with them, but the good news is that they "move on" before they can cause too much trouble. This group

89

is the in-between group who is groping to find their own identity. As a substitute teacher, your job is not to help them find their place in this world but to appreciate that they are going through this process and as a result might be rude and more confrontational than any other group. *Be prepared. Be strong, fair, calm, and creative.*

My next suggestion is simple. Remember when you were their age. Much has changed but much has remained the same. These years were difficult for us and, from personal observation, they still are. If ever there was a better opportunity for a substitute to keep a low profile, it is now. Don't make waves. Don't deviate from the lesson plan. Don't be over-friendly. Don't be anything except professional and fair.

Introduce yourself, simply, and offer "free time" vouchers to anyone who finishes the work you will assign. At this level you might want to lay out stacks of interesting seatwork, puzzles, riddles, and games as well as your stack of magazines and comic books.

If for any reason, your classroom is taken over by a student, "draw the noose." Few can withstand the temptation to play "Hangman" at this age, especially when you have chosen the words, "Czechoslovakia, Gypsy, and Antidisestablishmentarianism."

(Don't forget to pull out your "cheat sheet" or have your phone ready to Google any word in an instant so you spell the words correctly: You will most likely need it.)

These kids are not so sophisticated that they disdain stickers. Just make sure that they are cool "Biker Stickers" or something other than Disney (at least for the boys).

Preventing Disasters While Teaching Grades 9–12

Accept that you will not be accepted—at least not right away. Remember, as always, you were hired to keep peace in the classroom, to present the lesson plan you hope is there, or to create one out of thin air if it is not. Your other duty, if you accept it, is to appear in *control* of yourself as you attempt to manage, not necessarily to control, the class.

Before you take your coat off, write your name on the board to avoid the off-putting, "Who are you?" routine. As the students file in, keep busy. You can spoil your day right away by being too chatty or too accessible. Never will you have a better opportunity to lock up your valuables and your mouth. This age student is highly critical, until they know and respect you. Sadly, some will steal from you given the opportunity.

Review in your mind why you are here:

1. To take an accurate roll (absenteeism is rampant at this level).
2. To teach to a lesson plan (the teacher's or yours).
3. To manage the classroom appropriately.
4. To handle disturbances.
5. To correct all papers (check to make certain everyone turned in his/her work).
6. To make certain the classroom is left in order.
7. To leave a short, concise, honest and upbeat note about the day.

One of the most valuable tools in managing a class or in defusing bad situations is to appeal to the higher side of an offending student. If someone is habitually throwing a twit, make them feel important about themselves. Test them out: give them a privilege. "Hunter, would you take this note to the office?" He just might return a changed person!

Or, he might not return at all. (He will?)

Calming the Savage Breast

William Congreve, 1697, in his work The *Mourning Bride*, claims that music *"Hath charms to soothe a savage breast or to soften rocks or bend a knotted oak."*

Ignoring the rightness or wrongness of the use of the word "savage," you are pinch-hitting for these kids' teacher and need a "sure-fire" fix to soothe, soften, and bend the hearts and minds of the pupils in front of you, some overtly daring you to succeed.

Armed with your *Boom Box* and Carly *Simon's Coming Around Again, (Itsy Bitsy Spider)*, you have a fighting chance at soothing, softening, and bending your class.

The problem in the upper levels is that usually a portion (2/3) of any class is quietly going about the assignment while another portion (1/3) is bent on mayhem. Is it fair to play this song, possible disrupting those who are on task? (Yes, and I don't know.)

"Class, for the next 3 minutes and 43 seconds, I am going to play a song I like to play when some of us feel out of sorts. I would ask you to listen to the song and perhaps critique it for me. By that I don't mean to call out your feelings but to scribble a few impressions you have from listening to the words and the music that might be familiar to you. This is not mandatory; and if you are finished with your assignments, just chill."

In the lower grades I use this song to lead impromptu standing exercises or, in some cases to dance in place. If you have an assignment teaching PE or access to the gym, you can expand on this to have "free dance" or a game inspired by this inspiring song. Or, you might teach them to do the "Locomotion," or simple line-dancing steps to the music.

Another "too good too be true" song is "Respect Yourself," by the Staple Singers (Metro Lyric). I have changed three of the words to make this an acceptable sing along.

Respect Yourself*

If you disrespect anybody that you run into
How in the world do you think anybody's s'posed
to respect you?
If you don't give a heck 'bout a man with a *holy book*
in his hand, y'all
Just get out the way, and let the gentleman do his thing
You the kind of guy that want everything your way, yeah
Take that look off your face boy; it's a brand new day

Chorus
Respect yourself, respect yourself, respect yourself, respect
yourself
If you don't respect yourself
Ain't nobody going to give a good cahoot, na, na, na, na
Respect yourself, respect yourself, respect yourself,
respect yourself

If you're walkin' 'round thinkin' the world owes you
something cuz you're here
You goin' out the world backwards like you did
when you first come here, yeah
Keep talking keep talking 'bout the president won't s
top air pollution
Put your hand on your mouth when you cough,
that'll help the solution
Oh, you cuss around women and you don't even
know their names, no
Then you're dumb enough to think that'll make you
a big ol' man

Chorus

*Songwriters: Luther Thomas Ingram & Mack Rice; Lyrics: Universal
Music Pub. Group

93

Corrections

This will be short because I, as a sub, don't believe in punishments. I do, however, believe in diversion, defusing, and diagnostic efforts as shown on page 85 in the form of a questionnaire. If these efforts fail, then I believe in a correction, or an effort to give the student an assignment that is punitive in nature because it is repetitive. (Boring!)

I admit that there are some times when students need to cool their jets in this manner.

In grades 1–12, I suggest presenting them with a list of words to be copied down as many times as you feel their offense warrants. In first grade you may need to look through their reader to find words that are compatible with their level of achievement.

For grades 2–6, find where they are in their spelling book and prescribe the copying of each work as many times as you feel helpful to get hold of themselves.

For grades 6–12, go on-line to select words from their lists of "most often misspelled words" beginning with the word misspelled. Present them with a list of words you have pre-selected and give them the opportunity to choose eight words which they will write ten times. (Even though they are being "corrected," I like to give them a little pat on the head by allowing them to choose which words they will tackle.)

To add to this correction, you might ask the student to use each word they have chosen in a sentence. If you see that the student has calmed down and has done a good job on the work you assigned, how about a sticker or some "I Chilled Out" water? It's always good to clear the air and show that you understand their point of view.

But What About Me?

Before I begin Appendix 2, which will talk about books, songs, games, and dances, and before I describe novel art projects, seat games, story starters, rewards, and motivators, I'd like to turn to you, the teacher.

As in any profession there are going to be times that you are in "over-load." You handled or failed to handle one crisis too many. You are exhausted, spent. You wonder how you will get through the day, the week, month, the year? You have had it!

It's time to get centered. Let's hope that any personal melt-down happens close to a break in your day; but, if it doesn't, you can and should create your own Nirvana.

The first step is often enough to pull you together: **Practice deep breathing.** Even as you stand in front of your group you can, after a little practice, enjoy the cleansing effects of breathing deeply, the key to seamlessly gaining control of yourself. Here's how: (This is a combination of several exercises with a little yoga thrown it.)

1. Stand with your thumb and fore finger connected to make a circle; elbows facing front.

2. Exhale deeply through your nose to a count of 8. (Your nose is a good filter system.)

3. Hold that breath inside for a count of 5 or 6.

4. Exhale slowly but completely through your lips to a count of 8 or 9.

5. Repeat.

This exercise can be adapted to fit the situation. While listening to the class read or during their written spelling tests, you can practice this in full; but you can also tailor this exercise into other situations, even when you are interacting with your students.

Use your free time to get centered by five or six sets of deep breathing exercises and then launch into what Lucinda Bassett, in her national best seller titled *From Panic to Power,* discusses in Chapter Eight: "Compassionate Self-Talk: You Have to Be the One You Run to." The gist of this chapter is this: If you don't like yourself, who will? Be kind to yourself, build yourself up, be your own parachute, have options, have proud and happy memories, and have a strong faith that you nourish every way you can, every day.

Your mantra might be:

❀ I like me even when I mess up. I can do better, apologize, and forgive others and myself.

❀ I like to remember how far I've come. Remember when…?

❀ I like to recall times where I succeeded over enormous odds.

❀ I can control my reactions to any situation, no matter what.

❀ I will practice under-reacting to tense situations, conflict, and/or criticism.

❀ I will try to find humor in my day and view my students' behavior with understanding and compassion.

❀ I can incorporate deep-breathing into the day by teaching the technique to my students.

❀ I can choose to be negative or positive: choose a negative thought or a positive one.

❀ I will strive today and every day to be calm, fair, compassionate, strong, and happy.

❀ I can turn a disruptive class around with positive motivators and light-hearted fun.

❀ I will use music to soothe my day and that of my students.

❀ I will see exercise, a "fresh-air walk," or meditation as a good way to get centered.

❀ I will celebrate having survived this day tonight and have a better plan for tomorrow.

This is my list. What would yours look like? Why not load your iPod or your Smart Phone with positive strokes, comforting solutions, happy memories, and pictures to delight and divert you? Why not build yourself up? You know how good you are. Then, load your Boom Box with music you like. (Carly Simon's "Itsy Bitsy Spider?" That song and classical music soothed me during the latter part of my teaching career.)

Another important step in getting centered is to write about your feelings. Take the time to write every little detail about your discontent. Mention names, use profanity, allow yourself every opportunity to be small and inappropriate; to be "spiritually bank-rupt," hateful, spiteful, resentful, childish, nutty, whacked-out, negative, and irreverent. Then, safely save this "mirror of your despair" where you can read it later and laugh/cry.

"Scream therapy" is another technique I offer in an effort to get centered. Use a designated "scream pillow," and let your feelings rip while not disturbing the neighbors.

The last two suggestions are quieter and far more sedate. If your leanings are towards Christianity, I suggest a jewel of a book titled *Jesus Calling* by Sarah Young. It's a life-saver and small enough to drop into your purse or a jacket pocket. It feels good in your hands and in your heart and mind.

The last step to getting centered I will offer is meditation. There are thousands of ways to meditate and all of them are helpful. There are also CDs that provide a soothing musical background, some designed specifically for those wishing to meditate. Find a piece of music that you like to drown out any background noise. Put it in your TK for use at school. Use the timer also from your

TK set at ten minutes. Since the point is be free of stress, you will not likely relax if you have an eye towards waking up in time to conduct the rest of your day.

After you have done what you need to do to teach your class, set the timer.

1. Close the door, shut off the lights, and turn on your chosen music to a low volume.

2. Sit upright: back straight, arms loosely at your side again with thumb and forefinger making a circle. Cross your feet.

3. Close your eyes, enjoying the sensation of no sensation. (Use a sleep mask?)

4. Begin your deep breathing exercises, exaggerating each part, enjoying each phase, feeling more and more rested as you concentrate totally and fully on deep breathing.

5. Train yourself to think of nothing other than the sensation of deep breathing and the music you have chosen.

6. You may select a soothing word to repeat in your head to help you stay focused. At home you might try staring into a lighted candle when you have the luxury of time.

If you wish to visualize something specific, select a scene that you particularly enjoyed and focus on that scene. Rather than any memories the scene might invoke, notice the colors, the textures, the shadows, the light, and the tranquility the scene moves deep inside of you. Breathe the "air" the scene suggests and the feeling of total peace.

Looking good is a vital part of teaching school because looking good is a vital part of feeling good. And feeling good will make you a better person, a better teacher.

Little kids like bright colors on their teachers and big kids pay attention to brand names and current styles. Use your ingenuity to turn up with clothes even your students can understand and approve. You stand in front of a group of kids all day, everyday.

Know that they are reacting to what you look like as well as what you say and do. And, conversely, you are reacting to how they are reacting to you. Make this cycle positive.

Who wouldn't react better to a teacher who has a neat hairdo, looks sharp, and stands tall and straight rather than someone who looks thrown together and slumps in a chair?

Dress for success. Dress happy! Be happy; it's your choice. It always was.

Appendix 2

Resources

Symmetry at Work

Remember back in the preface, where I wrote about my seventy-eight-year-old friend who earned $300.00 a day, subbing for a junior high art class last spring?

Because I enjoy symmetry and Denna's company, I invited her to lunch to talk about this book and to "pick her agile brain." I wanted to end *Teaching School is a Scream* with a cutting edge.

Over pots of hot tea and Chinese food, we covered a lot of territory that August day. I learned that she is already letting those who call and assign subs know that she is available. She also advised them that she is interested in any long-term assignments that they might already know about. This is proactive subbing—something you should do. Let the folks at Human Resources Department know late in the summer that you are on the ball. Get ahead of the game and nail the long-term stints that they have already projected for teachers who are pregnant or have other plans requiring a dependable, eager sub—you!

While neither she nor I can promise you $300 a day, what you earn might even be more dependent on the school district and the length of your term. Make certain you inquire about the rates. Sadly, this too is something I failed to do and taught two months shy of a full year for substitute rates. Don't let that happen to you. If you learn one thing from this book, let it be this: MAKE CERTAIN THAT YOU ARE BEING PAID CORRECTLY. Ask questions. Compare rates within school districts. Rather than finding you "pushy," you will be seen as careful and efficient.

So far in this book I have prepared you to enter a classroom with no lesson plan provided or one that was written in haste.

My friend's recent experience in the one school system where she teaches is different. She signs in at the reception desk, is given a key to the classroom, a packet including the lesson plan, a roster, a lunch count sheet, and any other important information.

When she subs in Junior High (6–8), she also signs in at the reception office and is given the classroom key and a packet, although sometimes this information was emailed directly to her. She will have five one-hour classes and usually one hour for "planning." Normally, she will have a fifteen-minute break during recess as teachers in her district do not monitor recess. She will have a forty-five-minute lunch period. If there is a shortage of subs that day (this often happens), you might be asked to "cover" a class for another teacher. Be gracious. Your attitude, one way or another, will be remembered.

If she is teaching high school (grades 9–12), she is given a key and usually a packet. (As I write this, I need to remind you that accidents do happen, and there will be times when the teacher did not plan to be absent and did not leave a recognizable plan. Therefore, it behooves you to take to heart my advice on the subject and be capable of keeping the class busy with seatwork as you invent a fabulous lesson plan of your own.)

Due to the high and discouraging incidence of truancy today, many districts require teachers to send class-by-class attendance reports to the office. I never found this inconvenient as I got a chance to fit a face and a name together. It's amazing how quickly an experienced sub can remember a student's name and also "size up" their students. The "trouble makers" often stand out for you to love and inspire during your time together.

My friend then opened a more serious subject than truancy. Due to the violence and terrorism that has plagued our society and, in particular, our schools, those who work in schools are given specific information concerning this sensitive subject. Teachers and subs alike are expected to take classes and to be tested on the information that the school districts for which they work feel is important. While this may be disturbing, it is what you must do to keep your students and yourself safe and prepared for possible emergencies. It's important to know their codes, such as *code red.*

Kiddy Lit

In a more perfect world, I would be dashing off book title after book title and song after song for Pre K–5. In fact, that had been my initial plan but life got in the way.

Today, many school districts keep a tight control over the books a teacher may read or the songs that they may sing (with good reason, I think). It will be your responsibility to deal with this situation as soon as you can.

That's the bad news. The good news is that as a sub, you have access to books that are already on display in the classroom and in the library. Use some of your free time to chat with the school librarian to get a list of approved books and to look over which books that particular school finds acceptable. (Note, however, that many libraries don't loan books to subs so it is good to have your own mini library ready at all times.) Most public libraries have lists available of outstanding books selected by age groups, too. Or go on line and look at the "Caldecott Award books," my favorite source.

I wager that Dr. Seuss has made the cut, so purchasing a copy or two from his many adventures would be a safe investment, as would the purchase of the age-old classics, "Charlotte's Web" and the "Winnie-the-Pooh" series. Because your time with your students is usually limited, you would be wise to concentrate on short stories or simply ask your students if their "regular teacher" is reading them a story and if so, "What? And where is it?" Or, you could gather a few books from their book shelves and have them vote for the story they would like to hear. Add calm to their day and yours with a story read soothingly by you, their new, favorite substitute teacher?

Music

In our ever-changing world much has changed in the curriculum of Pre K–12. For openers, cursive writing is no longer taught. Music, art, library and physical education are often added to the week by a specialist in the field, leaving the full-time teacher some time to correct papers or plan. That's the good news. The bad news is that these classes are fun and can foster classroom cooperation and companionship, now a lost opportunity.

As a part-time teacher you will find that small doses of music, art, reading, or physical education can add greatly to the day and provide you with a tool to motivate and reward your students. Music, i.e., singing, is also an excellent way to let your students know that they are making too much noise or to alert them that "free time" is over and it's time to "clean-up." Singing a cheerful tune is a better signal than hearing a teacher try to scream over a classroom full of noisy students. Have the kids join you: Lift your arms and sing!

But, before you sing a note, find out the school's policy regarding music. Ask the teachers you meet in the lounge what songs they sing, if any, with their students. It's always better to be safe than sorry. Google to find a myriad of wonderful songs, some with music. Here are a few of my favorite tunes, shortened to make them teachable:

Little Boy Blue (Pre-K–3)

Little boy blue come blow your horn.
The sheep's in the meadow; the cow's in the corn.
Where is the boy who looks after the sheep?
He's under the haystack, fast asleep.

♫

Baa Baa Black Sheep (Pre-K–2)

Baa, baa black sheep
have you any wool?
Yes sir, yes sir
three bags full.
One for my master
and one for my dame
and one for the little girl
who lives down the lane.

♫

London Bridge (Pre-K–3)

London Bridge is falling down,
falling down, falling down.
London Bridge is falling down,
my fair lady.
Build it up with sticks and stones,
sticks and stones,
sticks and stones.
Build it up with sticks and stones,
my fair lady-eo!

♫

Doggy in the Window (Pre-K–4)

How much is that doggy in the window?
The one with the waggely tail?
How much is that doggy in the window?
I do hope that dog is for sale.
I must take a trip to California,
and leave my poor sweetheart alone.
If she has a little dog she won't be lonesome
and the doggy would have a good home.

Old Mother Hubbard (Pre-K–2)

Old Mother Hubbard
went to the cupboard
to get her poor doggy a bone,
but when she got there
the cupboard was bare
the poor little doggy had none.

♫

ABC Song (Pre-K–3)

A, B, C, D,
E, F, G,
H, I, J, K,
L, M, N, O, P,
Q, R, S, T,
U, V,
W and X,
Y, Z
Tell me what you
think of me.
I can say my ABC's!

♫

The Itsy Bitsy Spider (Pre-K–4)

The itsy bitsy spider
climbed up the waterspout.
(Touch index finger to opposing thumb, raising arms.)
Down came the rain
(Hold hands up, wiggle fingers and slowly lower arms.)
and washed the spider out.
(Make swishing movements, side to side.)

Out came the sun
(Hands meet over head to make a circle.)
and dried up all the rain
and the itsy, bitsy, spider climbed up the spout again.
(Thumb/index action again.)

♫

I'm a Little Teapot (Pre-K–2)

I'm a little teapot, short and stout
Here is my handle. *(Arm on hip.)*
Here is my spout.
(Other arm bent at elbow, to resemble spout.)
When you want some tea
just tip me over and
pour it out. *(Bend sideways.)*

♫

Wheels on the Bus (Pre-K–3)

The wheels on the bus go round and round
round and round, round and round.
The wheels on the bus go round and round
all… day… long.

Get creative and add your own items on the bus and the noise they make. Do this as a group and draw a picture of the addition for little ones or write the words on the board.

The wipers/swish, swish, swish
The horn/honk, honk, honk

The baby on the bus/wah, wah, wah
The bee on the bus/buzz, buzz, buzz
The driver/hush, hush, hush

This is an extremely exciting song and can run a long time before interest wanes.

♫

If You're Happy and You Know it (Pre-K–5)

This song gives you another chance to involve your kids in choosing words and actions.

If you're happy and you know it, clap your hands.
If you're happy and you know it, clap your hands.
If you're happy and you know it, and you really want to show it.
If you're happy and you know it, clap your hands.

Have a contest to find more action:

"If you're happy and you know it, wiggle your nose."
"If you're happy and you know it, clear your throat."

Have fun with the possible options.
Note: YouTube has a wealth of children's songs and many of them also have the words.

Seatwork

Let's begin with seatwork, because without it your day will be toast. For those who don't know, seatwork can be crossword puzzles, mazes, Sudoku, word searches, word games, pages to color, jokes, riddles, maps, "Treasure Hunts," and so much more.

Sometimes, if the teacher knows he/she will be absent, he/she will have put out some seatwork. If not, you should come prepared to run off copies from your own stash.

Go on-line to find sources for these "life savers." I find that Dollar Tree, Inc. has a surprisingly good selection of materials geared to teachers. If it does not have what you need or want, you can refer to their catalog, and the materials will be sent to your nearest Dollar Tree store. *Under no circumstances should you copy any material that is copyrighted or not intended to be copied. You could get into terrible trouble as a result.*

And, be aware that children who belong to the Jehovah's Witness Church must not be handed seatwork that smacks of any holidays.

Why is seatwork important? The beginning of each day can be hectic and noisy as students saunter in and greet one another while you are trying to set your course for the day. Yet, when they see some interesting material lying on their desk, most students tend to spend their time working on it rather than socializing or causing trouble.

Unfinished seatwork can be used as filler should students finish their assignment early or have free time. I often offer prizes for the best seatwork in several different categories: neatest, most eye-appealing, most accurate, whatever you can find to admire. Everyone loves to be appreciated or at least recognized for their good work.

Story Starters

Another form of seatwork is the use of "Story Starters." Entice the class into a writing contest choosing from ideas you write on the board: make them interesting and geared to the age group you are teaching. Here are some samples:

- "My Mom just won the Publishers' Clearing House contest and we are going to get ten thousand dollars every month for life. She wants me to make a list of all the things I would like to buy and do. Here's my list."

- "I have been chosen as 'Principal for the Day.' What am I going to change during this time?"

- "If I could visit any place on earth, where would I like to go and why?"

- "What do I like about school? What do I not like about school?

- Describe your favorite book, movie or TV program in detail. Why did you like it?

- Who is your favorite person, living or dead, and why do you like them?

- If your dreams come true, what will you be doing twenty years from now.

- What do you look for in a friend? What annoys you in a "friend?

- Would you like to take a trip into space? Why? or Why not?

- What is the most exciting thing that ever happened to you? The most challenging? The happiest? The most embarrassing? The funniest?

Prizes

I enjoy awarding prizes to stimulate and reward good work or behavior. It used to be a very simple task to hand out Jelly Beans or Gummy Bears. Today that would be unwise for many reasons, the most important being allergies or the possibility of choking.

Again, you can go on-line to purchase items you consider appropriate. I find what I need at a Dollar Tree where I buy a wide variety of stickers and cute erasers.

And then, there is my special prize usually given out to a student who was having a bad day but turned it around and cooperated. That prize is carefully chosen, and unless there is someone allergic to bottled water, I am hitting a home run when I pass out one of my small bottles of water with a teacher-made label saying: "I chilled out!" or "I'm way cool." Have the labels on a bottle or two and store them in the refrigerator in the teachers' lounge in the morning. Take them out during lunch break and keep them hidden, hoping that in the afternoon you will find someone totally deserving. Compose your own label, or just write the student's name. I buy this water at a Dollar Tree, as well.

But you don't have to go to such elaborate measures to reward good work. I can still remember how pleased my classmates and I were to come in from recess and see our spelling test on the board boasting a beautiful sticker. Kids still feel that way until fifth grade. After that, you can still reward good work by writing a brief comment in red pen.

A smallish investment on your behalf might be the game of "BINGO." You might go on-line or even make your own game. After subbing for a while, you will see the beauty of doing something that creates harmony, fun, and cooperation. BINGO!

A very simple way to play a game is by guessing. As the teacher, you can get the attention of the class by giving your first clue: "I am thinking of something in this room."

Students are encouraged to *raise their hands* to ask for a

clue. "Is it large?" In grades 2–12, write on the board, "Large. No." Continue until someone guesses. This game is a sneaky way of painlessly teaching language arts. Even "big kids" like to play (usually).

Or you might focus this game on a person. You might name a category such as presidents, movie stars, famous athletes, or rock stars. Steer clear of games that center on fellow students. Feelings might be hurt in this contest, at least after the PK-K years.

You might even have an old-fashioned Spelling Bee. Have the students pull out their spelling books and "study up" for a few minutes. Then divide the room in half and go student by student on each side to spell a word from next week's spelling test.

Another nifty idea is a memory game. Begin by saying "I am going on a trip. In my suitcase I will pack my tablet." Student must remember what has gone before them and then add something of their own. If the student forgets something, they lose their turn and the next student takes up the challenge. It's okay to write the items down, but the game gets pretty fast-paced and is a better challenge if items are only memorized.

Games

Of course you recognize that Madonna is a "Material Girl." But, you have no way of knowing, until now, that I am not only a "Material Girl" (I love to sew), but I am an "Inside Girl," and a card-carrying "Non-Jock."

I hated recess, even when I was a student. I hated it a lot more as a teacher freezing in the cold, sopping wet in the rain, sweltering in the heat, or suffering from allergies in the fall and spring. Yet, I did my best to stand guard or to provide an outdoor activity that was fun and safe. I also was called upon, often, to teach PE indoors. I will give you some ideas for each contingency, although I am happy to remind you that many school districts do not expect their teachers to do recess duty or to teach PE, ever!

Relays

Relays are probably the best game to suggest as you can do this with students indoors or out of doors. You will need two teams. The teacher taps or points to each student saying "Team A or B." You need a whistle and a scarf for each side. (These items are in your TK?)

1. Line up teams, side by side (no pushing, shoving, or messing around or you're out).

2. The first person on each team takes a scarf and, after the whistle, runs to and back from a designated spot. TEAMS MUST HAVE EVEN NUMBER OF RUNNERS.

3. When they return to the line, they "hand over" the scarf to the next runner.

4. That runner repeats the run, returns and hands over the scarf to the next runner.

5. The winning team is the side whose runners have each completed their relay.

Work-Up

This is a baseball game usually played outside. You can use a large number of students but usually a team of 15 students is best. You might divide your students into two teams if there's room. This game was something every kid used to understand and was played in a neighborhood setting or on the front lawn of an indulgent parent. The rules take getting used to because it is a rotation game in which every player has a chance to excel. Equipment: softball, softball bat(s), four bases made of filled sacks, boards, rocks, or cardboard. Pitcher's plate (optional) marked with chalk or a dab of red poster paint.

The Lineup

1. Batters: Those left after you have "manned" your team. Ideally no more than five.

2. Left field

3. Center field

4. Right field

5. Third base

6. Second shortstop

7. Second base

8. First shortstop

9. First base

10. Pitcher

11. Catcher

Each batter tries to hit the ball and run to a base. If he/she strikes out or gets tagged, he/she replaces the left fielder who moves to the batter lineup. Everyone moves up one position. Batters strike out, are put out at bases, put out when a fly ball is caught or if the pitcher beats them to any base or home plate.

Seven Up

This game is an inside/outside game played alone or with no more than three. You need a small, soft rubber ball and a wall or hard surface against which to bounce the ball.

The idea here is to perform a set of actions and when you drop the ball or miss the ball you forfeit your turn, and the next person plays. If playing alone, start over.

1. Throw the ball in the air seven times and catch it.

2. Throw the ball against a wall six times; let it bounce one

time before catching it.

3. Throw the ball against a wall and catch it five times without bouncing it.

4. Throw the ball against a wall and turn around catching it four times.

5. Throw the ball against a wall, turn around, and clap before catching it three times.

6. Throw the ball under your leg against the wall and catch it two times.

7. Throw the ball under your leg against the wall and clap one time.

This is my version but you can design your own to suit your age group appropriately.

Dances

I love to dance and I loved to introduce students to moving with music as a PE session. To fully understand what I am attempting to explain, please go online and look up "How to do the Locomotion, accompanied by Little Eva." Then, look up Carly Simon's fabulous song "Coming' Around Again," which features a bit of "Itsy Bitsy Spider."

Locomotion

You will need a copy of Little Eva's song and your *Boom Box* if your gym doesn't have its own sound system. The simplest way to handle this dance is to form two lines and hold on to the person directly in front of you. Listen to the music and do whatever it says, dropping your grip on the person in front of you as necessary.

Okay, it's going to be a little wild but it's a lot of fun. Or, you might prefer a more controlled version with older students. Stand in front of them and demonstrate what moves you wish them to copy. I suggest that you turn around so that they are mimicking your moves. Make them simple at first. Eventually some of your students will be better than you at *doin' the locomotion*. The dance is fun and gets better with time and practice.

Coming Around Again/Itsy Bitsy Spider

I am glad to conclude this section on such a happy note with a dance routine that is certain to delight teacher and student alike. You will need Carly's song, but I've mentioned that before and I mean it!

This is best done in a gym but it is okay outside or in the classroom in a modified version.

In a gym or outside, to go for extra drama, use crepe paper streamers eight feet long, rolled up, at first with rubber bands. (For more drama, attach crepe paper to a straw.)

Line the students up facing you in a side-by-side line or two lines, one in front of the other. Hand out the crepe paper. Instruct the students to put the rubber bands around their wrists and unroll the paper. Standing in place, move your arms in a figure eight in time to the music.

When the song reverts to "Itsy Bitsy Spider," have the students put the crepe paper around their necks and proceed with the hand gestures outlined on pages 119-120.

At the end of the song, allow free dancing with or without the crepe paper. By this time you and your students are pretty much into the spirit of this wonderful song.

Suggested dance moves done in place: Feet together, right foot goes behind left and bend, slightly. Return right foot and put left foot behind right foot and bend slightly. Twist arms to music. Good moves for "Coming Around Again" or many other songs.

"Easy" Art for Elementary School

The projects I will describe are those I found to be the most successful with K-5. Beyond that level, art, if it is offered at all is a class you choose to gain a credit.

Toilet Paper Carnations

Materials:

- Two (2) inexpensive rolls of white toilet paper (Please note that expensive toilet paper is more difficult to work with.)
- White pipe cleaners
- Green colored paper

Steps:

1. Tear and stack 10 pieces of toilet paper with the jagged ends all in one direction.
2. Fold back and forth with jagged ends out.
3. Fasten with pipe cleaner; leave long "stem."
4. Gently pull jagged ends toward you to fashion a carnation.
5. Trace leaves. Cut them out.
6. Punch a hole in the center and slide in the pipe cleaner leaving a long stem.

Panda Bear

Materials:
- One white, one black colored paper (12" x 9")
- 7" paper plate
- Mason jar lids. (Always carry in TK for kids to borrow to help them cut round shapes)
- Scrap of pink to use as nose and "pad" on Panda's feet
- Scrap of gray to line ears
- White triangle or dots from paper punch for eye highlights
- Red, black marker
- Glue
- Scissors

Steps:
1. Cut out face using plate.
2. Attach to torso: centered and 2.5" down from top.
3. Tracing outside of Mason jar lid cut 6 circles of white and four of black.
4. Tracing inside of lid cut 2 pink and two gray circles.
5. Using spool of thread trace 2 black eyes and one red mouth.
6. Assemble, glue and draw on mouth and eyelashes.
7. Attach white triangles or punched out paper on eyes.

Winnie the Pooh

Materials:

- Two brown pieces of colored paper, 12" x 9"
- Half sheet of red
- Scraps of light-yellow for paws and deeper yellow for honey
- Blue, green or gray for honey pot
- Scrap of pink for tongue
- Scrap of black for eyes and nose
- White dots from paper punch for eyes
- Paper plate
- Mason jar lids
- Glue
- Scissors
- Black marker

Steps:

1. Lightly fold brown paper and slice off slant at approximately 8" from top.
2. Lay 1/2 sheet of red paper on top to trace around for sweater. (Trim bottom: Optional.)
3. Using paper plate, cut out face.
4. Trace 6 circles on brown paper using outside of jar lids.
5. Trace four light-yellow circles using inside of jar lid.
6. Using deeper yellow scrap cut out circle 4" in diameter. Circle doesn't need to be perfect as it fits into "pot."
7. Using plate again, trace two circles for the honey pot.
8. Glue circle on Pooh's tummy, 1/2" up from the bottom and centered.
9. Cut upper third of second circle and glue circumference leaving top open.

10. Glue on eyes, nose, ears, arms, feet and "linings."

11. Using marker, draw on eyebrows, mouth; highlight feet and ears.

12. Fashion a pink tongue from scraps and glue in place.

13. Write Pooh's name across his red sweater and write "Honey" on the honeypot.

OPTIONAL: Fashion a bee to hover around the honey pot.

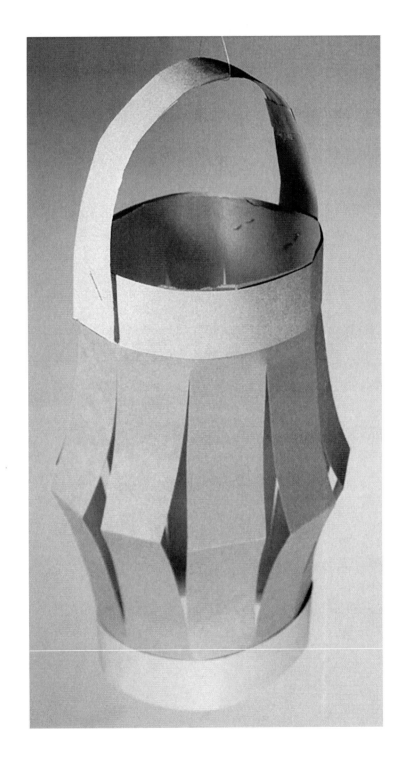

Halloween Pumpkin
(Super easy project.)

Materials:

- One orange and one black piece (to be shared) 12" x 9" colored paper
- Stapler
- Scissors
- Scraps of yellow paper for eyes and mouth. (Optional.)

Steps:

1. Lightly fold orange paper in half, lengthwise.
2. Slice (cut) in 1" intervals to within 1/12" of raw edge.
3. Staple: Preferable to gluing.
4. Cut three 1/2" strips from black or green: One for top trim, one for bottom trim and one for lantern handle.
5. Use yellow scraps to make "scary" eyes and mouth.

NOTE: Glue can be used in lieu of stapler but not recommended.

Skeleton
(Easy/quick!)

Materials:

- Three pieces of 12" x 9" gray or white colored paper
- One piece of 17.5" x 12" for background
- Black and red marker

Steps:

1. Cut torso to measure 9" x 6". Cut two 9" x 2" strips for arms; two 12" x 2" for legs.

2. Use plate to trace round head. Fold, lightly and make indentation with pattern (Teacher assist necessary with sketch on board and/or sample.)

3. Cut one 8"x 1.5" strip in black and four 3/4" strips for ribs. Glue in place.

4. Glue arms and legs securely. Glue skull 1/2" down from torso top.

5. Get creative with marker: Look at sample and draw in bones, teeth and scar.

6. Fold up feet and hands and add more bones.

7. Cut out two eyes from thread spool and fashion an oval "nose hole."

8. Glue and write "BOOOOOO!"

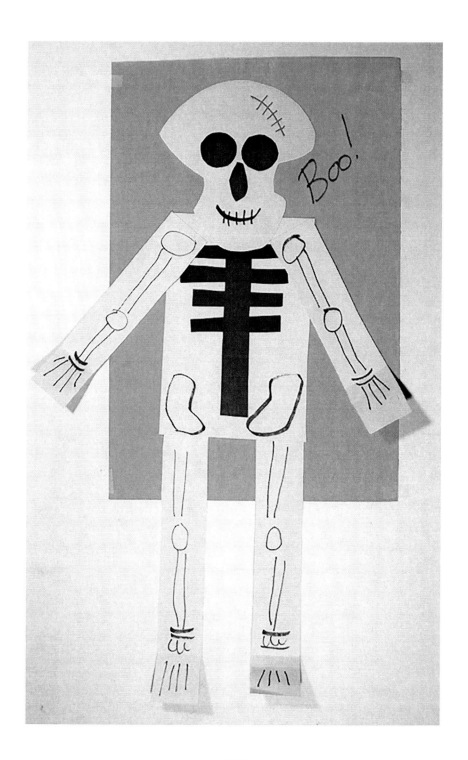

126

Valentine

Easy!

Materials:

- Three pieces of 12" x 9" red colored paper
- Chalk for each student
- Several valentine patterns to share (Some find the shape difficult to do.)
- Marker
- Stapler or glue
- White scraps for hands and feet; black and pink scraps for eyes and mouth

Steps:

1. Fold red paper lengthwise and use pattern to draw half valentine.

2. Cut two 12" x 3" strips for legs and two 6" x 3" for arms. Fold accordion style. Glue.

3. Using pattern, cut four hearts for hands and feet. Glue or staple.

4. Using thread spool cut two while eyes and tiny hearts or circles to go inside. Add white dot from paper punch. Cut small hearts for mouth or use spool to make circles.

Directions for "I've Got a Cold in my Head," are in Chapter 6: "A Sure Fire Art Project."

Toy Soldiers

This project is time intensive but worth it,
especially around Christmas

**This project to be glued to 2 pieces of
17.5" by 12" colored paper.**

Materials:

- 2 pieces of red: 1 for torso and 1 for arms
- 3 pieces of black for legs, strap and hat
- One pink piece of colored paper for face and hands
- 1/2" piece yellow for epaulets and belt buckle
- a scrap of brown paper for two "boots"
- Paper plate to share: 7" diameter
- Mason Jar lid to used to trace circles
- Spools of thread to share in designing mouth and eyes
- Scraps of blue, brown, black and white for eyes, red for mouth
- Glue
- Scissors
- Marker (This project is time intensive but worth it, especially around Christmas)

Steps:

1. Glue two pieces of 17.5" x 12" colored paper as background. (Necessary!)

2. Cut out face from pink paper using paper plate as pattern.

3. Cut one inch off red paper for torso.

4. Lightly fold black paper, lengthwise and cut off at 7".

5. Use chalk to draw curve for top of helmet. (Teacher should draw pattern on board.)

6. Cut "legs" 3 inches wide and 9 inches long.

7. Use brown scraps to cut circles for "boots" tracing outside of Mason jar lid.

8. Cut 2" circles for hands using pink paper, tracing outside of Mason jar lid.

9. Cut three 3" x 3" squares: two for epaulets and one for belt buckle.

10. Cut strap from black paper: 12" x 1.5" and belt 9" x 3".

11. Glue top part of torso leaving space free to fasten legs.

12. Cut out "boots" from brown scrap and glue to legs.

13. Place legs under torso and glue.

14. Glue buckle to belt and glue on soldier 5-1/4" from "shoulder" of torso.

15. Cut out pink "hands" tracing with jar lid. Attach to arms.

16. Glue arms.

17. Attach face, eyes and nose; Draw mouth and finish eyes. Optional.*

18. Use scissors to "fringe" epaulets. Glue them on.

19. Glue on helmet.

* To put sparkle in simple round-dot eyes, cut a smaller circle of black for each eye and a triangle or a dot of white paper from a paper punch. (This is worth the effort, every time.)

Author's Note

Cause and Effect

After much thought, I have decided that a statement I made should not remain in the readers' heart or mind as the most important take-away from this book. I wrote: If there is one thing you should remember from what I have written, it is that you should be certain that you are being paid properly.

Of course that is important. In fact, it's a given. But, the most important thought I want any reader to take from this book does not deal with you, the teacher. Instead, it deals with the necessity to begin teaching children, from the moment their tiny feet enter the classroom, the importance of cause and effect—that there are dire consequences for selfish behavior.

When we were stationed in Thailand, I went with a church group to "see a living saint." It was a long, hot, and typically dangerous drive far into the countryside.

The church where the "saint" served was small and unadorned. The priest was not striking except for the fact that his hair was white and his face was unlined. His Mass was not unusual, but his sermon was an electric shock for me—a lightening bolt, in fact.

"I am going to make my homily brief," he said, giving no reason. "I am going to tell you what the origin of sin is." I shifted in the pew thinking that what he outlined would be less than a brief discussion.

"All sin is selfishness and all selfishness is sin," he said. "If you can think of a sin, a criminal act or any bad behavior that isn't based on selfishness, I want you to let me know."

I want our kids to appreciate how entwined the relationship of cause and effect is to selfishness. I want them to know that in large measure, cause and effect will determine the success of their lives. That cause-and-effect training helps them make good choices, every day, all day. We need to train our students again and again to think from the stark perspective that reveals self-interest for what it is: a poisonous dead end.

If we constantly reinforced cause and effect and encouraged students to use these teachings as their private yardstick, would there be disciplinary problems in school? Would there be truancy? Would there be terrible high-speed car accidents? Would there be drugs, alcohol or cigarette use? Would there be bullying, sex, pregnancies or STD?

How can we make the subject appealing? With teacher-generated games, "What If's?" By reading biographies of great people who have surmounted incredible odds. By watching movies glorifying heroism instead of violence. By dialoging and taking Cause and Effect courses designed by experts who will adapt information appropriate at every level, PK–12. Do not say, "We don't have time." We have to make time for our kids to succeed.

This book is dedicated to a lady I didn't like very much until she rescued me the day before graduation by finding the missing credit the registrar claimed I still owed.

Dr. Ruth Willard was a relentless teacher, totally wrapped up in her profession, that of preparing elementary school teachers.

She used to deduct one grade for each spelling error. (Yes, it was possible to "go in the hole," I know.) Her hand-ins were famous for the breadth and depth of research required to properly address her expectations. It was easy to resent her then, as bleary-eyed you piled your work into a wheelbarrow to turn it in for her meticulous scrutiny.

But that was that and now is now and Ms. Willard is gone. She committed suicide in 1970 while we were stationed in Germany. I could not honor her with my presence then but I do so now.

I do not know why she ended her life or how. I only look back in sorrow to see a woman who gave us everything she had. Did we drain her? Did she feel appreciated? Fulfilled?

Formally, in Ms. Willard's honor I am throwing out the challenge to smart people everywhere to spearhead a movement toward making cause and effect an essential part of how we teach. Let us admit that cause and effect has driven every aspect of our universe from prehistoric times until today. Let us appreciate the impact cause and effect, (if I do this, this might happen; or if I do that, that might happen) has on our on our environment, our health, our commerce, our relationships, our social and our athletic interactions, our mental and physical well-being, and our search for meaning in life and death.

Simply put, I want cause and effect to be the way we learn, the way we teach, the means we use to pass on that which we know to be important and true.

Dr. Ruth A. Willard would understand. May she rest in peace.

About the Author

Judy Woods-Knight grew up in Salem, Oregon, where her father became Deputy State Forester. Her dad could "see into the souls of others," but Judy says that his overwhelming attributes were his generosity and his subtle sense of humor.

Her mother was a talented pianist, decorator, and cook. It was through 50 years of her weekly letters that Judy discovered the source of any writing skills she possesses today.

Her life as an Army wife and mother showed her the world and introduced her to a wide range of experiences, joys, stresses, and sorrows.

When reading this book, one can easily see the influences of her upbringing and her marriage and how they impacted her skills as a generous, flexible substitute teacher who always seemed to want to create win-win situations for her students and herself, regardless of how challenging any particular student may have been.

She now says, "If I were to sum up what I have learned in life it would be this: *"Everything is going to be fine in the end. If it's not fine, it's not the end"* (~ Oscar Wilde).